Brain and obsession

Mohammad Nabizadeh

ISBN:979-8-89372-711-1

CONTENTS

FOREWORD

In this book, obsessive-compulsive disorder (OCD) is examined with a neuro-psychological and biological approach. In this regard, attention has been paid to bring the latest researches and studies in the field of genetics, neurotransmitters, nervous-brain system in causing obsessive-compulsive disorder in this work. Animal models and pharmacology of obsessive-compulsive disorder have also been studied. in this book Since most of these researches and studies, directly or indirectly, have investigated the role of the complex and mysterious system of the human brain in creating OCD, the title of this work was chosen as "Brain and Obsession".

Mohammad Nabizadeh
Master of Science in Psychology, University
of Isfahan , Iran
November 2023

INTRODUCTION

The human brain is the manifestation of one of the greatest wonders of the world, and its function is an example of the greatest and most coherent functional systems of nature. Accurate understanding of brain function requires science that cannot be summarized in a single field. Scientists in various fields of neuroscience including anatomy, pharmacology, physiology, biochemistry, psychology, linguistics and artificial intelligence, have tried in some way to reveal part of the secrets of this precise and complex device to the extent of their knowledge.

What seems important in the meantime is that the researchers do not limit themselves to their general or specialized information and open the way for a better understanding of the functioning of the nervous system by studying more and more. In the current era, when sometimes writers write less than they should and readers may be less interested in reading detailed books, translation and authoring of books by the researchers who are determined to step into the wonderful world of brain functions deserves praise and admiration.

This book is the result of Mohammad Nabizadeh's perseverance and interest , who is a master's graduate in psychology, faculty of psychology, Isfahan University, Iran , It was prepared with his constant efforts and with the encouragement of his professors, and it is a review of the latest findings of neuroscience in the field of obsession. As a neuroscience researcher, I recommend reading this book to all interested people, especially psychiatry and psychology students.

Dr. Karim Asgari

PhD in behavioral pharmacology, associate
professor of Isfahan University, Iran

1 SYMPTOMS OF OBSESSIVE-COMPULSIVE DISORDER (OCD)

Bernice was 46 years old when she came for treatment, this was her fourth outpatient treatment and he had been hospitalized twice before. Her obsessive-compulsive disorder began twelve years ago, shortly after her father's death. Since then, this disorder has undergone minor and major changes.

Bernice's preoccupation was a fear of contamination, a fear she associated with her father's death from pneumonia. Although she stated that he was afraid of almost everything because the possibility of microbes was everywhere, she was particularly afraid of touching wood, rough objects, postal packages, canned goods, and silver particles such as silver writing on postal cards, eyeglass frames, shiny objects and silverware. She was unable to explain the possible contamination of these particular objects. To alleviate her distress, Bernice engages in obsessive activities that fill her waking hours almost entirely. In the mornings, she spent three to four hours in the bathroom, washing herself frequently. In the intervals between bathing, she rubs the edge of his soap dish so much to make sure that it is free of microbes. Her mealtimes also took hours, Bernice had certain eating habits—eating three bites at a time and chewing three hundred times, in her view it helped decontamination of food. Even her husband sometimes participated in these eating rituals and by shaking the teapot and frozen vegetables on Bernice's head to remove the microbes. Bernice's obsessive habits and fear of contamination had completely paralyzed her life; she didn't leave the house, didn't do the housework, and didn't talk to anyone on the phone (Davison et al. 2004).

The basic features of obsessive-compulsive disorder (OCD) are the symptoms of mental and practical obsessions that are severe enough to cause significant discomfort to a person. Thoughtful and practical obsessions are time-consuming and clearly interfere with daily and occupational performance, usual social activities or personal relationships. A patient with OCD may have an obsession , a compulsion, or a combination of them. An obsession is an intrusive and recurring thought, feeling, belief or sensation.

A compulsion is a self-conscious, regulated, and repetitive behavior, such as counting or avoidance. An Obsession increases a person's anxiety, while doing a compulsion reduces a person's anxiety. Overall, when a person resists doing a compulsion, his anxiety increases. A person with obsessive-compulsive disorder usually understands the irrationality of their obsessive thoughts. Both obsessions and compulsions are known to be ego-dystonic for the patient.

Although the compulsion may be help to reduce the anxiety associated with the obsessive thought, this is not always the case. Completing the compulsive action may not lead to the elimination of anxiety and may even increase it. Anxiety also appears when a person resists an compulsion (Sadock et al ,2007)

Obsessive-compulsive disorder is a disorder that appears to be diagnosed and treated in all age groups (Herbenson, 2009). Research shows that OCD affects two to three percent of the population (Gournay, 2006; Zepf, 2004).

This disorder is often associated with other psychological disorders such as depression, panic attacks, generalized anxiety, which complicates the treatment of this disease. (Keeley, Storch, Merlo &Geffken, 2008).

Obsession is having unwanted thoughts, imaginations or impulses that repeatedly and persistently enter the conscious mind of a person and cause anxiety. Practical obsession is an irresistible compulsion to do certain things or rituals that reduce anxiety. Obsessive thoughts are often accompanied by compulsions (for example: the thought of microbes remaining, accompanied by the compulsion to wash dishes several times before using them).The main element in this disorder is the feeling of lack of authority and lack of control, repetitive content, whether it is a thought (obsession) or an action (practical obsession/ compulsion), the patient tries to get rid of disturbing thoughts or compulsion to do repetitive tasks, but is unable to do that.

We all occasionally have these repetitive thoughts (for example, the thought that maybe I didn't turn off the gas stove when I left the house?), or get drawn to perform certain ritualistic behaviors (writing down a list of steps to complete a task). But in the case of someone suffering from obsessive-compulsive disorder, such thoughts and pulls are so time-consuming that they severely disrupt his daily life. The person himself knows that these thoughts and actions are irrational, but he cannot ignore them or put them aside. These people understand that obsessive behaviors are meaningless, but when they resist doing obsessive actions, they experience anxiety, and by doing them, they get relief from tension and torment.

The content of obsessive thoughts is very diverse. But they are often defined around harm to oneself or others, fear of contamination, and hesitation about ending work (Hilgard et al, 2014)

It is also interesting to note that the content of obsessions varies depending on the period of life. In ancient times, the theme of obsessive thoughts was religion and sexual matters: blasphemous thoughts or the impulse to shout blasphemies in the church or expose one's penis to everyone. Today, such obsessions are less common, and instead of contamination obsessions about syphilis or AIDS is a matter of fear of contamination.

Some obsessives have persistent thoughts but no repetitive actions.However; the majority of obsessives suffering from repetitive thoughts also have obsessive behavior. Obsessive behaviors are also very diverse, and washing and checking are among the most common of these behaviors.

"Washers" are those who, when facing certain objects or thoughts, feel contaminated and spend hours on washing and cleaning rituals. "Inspectors" check doors, lights, ovens, or the correctness of things ten, twenty, or a hundred times, or those who repeat things many times with certain rituals and believe that ritual behavior prevents catastrophic events or punishment. Sometimes ceremonial behavior is directly related to anxiety-provoking obsessions (such as repeatedly checking that the stove valve is closed to avoid a fire), some behaviors are not logically related to obsessions (repeatedly putting on and taking off clothes in order to prevent an accident for the child). The fundamental issue in all these repetitive behaviors is doubt. Obsessives can't trust their feelings or judgement, even when they see something is not dirty, or the door is locked, they still don't trust their eyes.

The common thing between obsessive compulsive disorder and panic disorder is that in both of these disorders, a person has severe anxiety and it is possible for a person to suffer from both disorders. At the same time, there are important differences between these two disorders. A panicked person rarely ruminates or ritualizes their fears. Their motivations are also different. Obsessive preoccupations such as being dirty, microbes and harming others rarely cause problems for people suffering from fear.

Obsessive-compulsive disorder often manifests itself at a young age. Obsession becomes chronic if not treated. Obsessive thoughts are very disturbing and obsessive behaviors are very time-consuming and maladaptive (repeated washing of hands until they bleed).In this way, people with this disorder are very disturbed psychologically(Hilgard et al, 2014)

Compulsion is a behavior that is followed by an obsession. These practical obsessions are done to make you feel better and get rid of worry. A person usually knows that obsessive actions are unnecessary and perhaps illogical, and this state often creates a lot of desperation and incapacity in the person. Compulsions are actions such as washing hands or checking the door too often. But sometimes these actions can be in your mind, for example counting sets of seven for seven minutes. The important thing is that these people know they have to do compulsions/obsessive actions. Even if you know what you're doing is stupid, you still can't resist doing that compulsive act if necessary. (Brosan et al., 2010).From a clinical point of view, the most common obsessions are fear of contamination, fear of sexual impulses or aggression, or hypochondria fears about body malpractice. Furthermore, mental obsessions may appear in the form of doubt, laziness and procrastination, and excessive indecisiveness. On the one hand, obsessive thinking is like the phenomenon of worry, which is a well-known feature of generalized anxiety disorder (GAD). This type of thinking is full of "what if...". Excessive worries with a ruminative nature about the possibility of unlikely negative events. The difference between these two types of thinking is that the person suffering from OCD considers their thoughts to be "alien" or "ego-dystonic", that is, they consider these thoughts to be issues that are imposed on them from the outside and do not have much meaning.On the contrary, a person with GAD is able to make logical statements about his concern and justify it, for example; think to ourselves: My child is late, so it is possible that he has been kidnapped. Otherwise, if obsessive thinking is justified (which are the case for 5% of cases) and if obsessive behavior is not visible, it is possible that we are dealing with a delusional disorder and maybe even schizophrenia.

Commonly reported practical obsessions/compulsions include: striving for cleanliness and order, sometimes through elaborate and unnecessary rituals that last for hours or even a large part of the day. Avoiding certain objects, such as anything brown, starting to do repetitive, magical and protective tasks such as counting, performing certain numbers, carrying a charm or touching a certain part of the body. Checking, repeated evaluations to make sure that previous tasks have been implemented correctly. For example, the light, gas valve, or water tap is closed, the window is not open, and the door is locked or performing a specific action, such as eating very slowly.

The most common result of obsessive-compulsive disorder is its adverse effect on a person's relationships with others, especially with family members. Relatives of the OCD including spouse, children, friends or colleagues, may feel uncomfortable or even disgusted by observing the patient's unending and irresistible need to repeatedly wash his hands every minute, wipe the door handle, or count the tiles on the bathroom floor. These belligerent feelings are probably mixed with feelings of guilt, because they understand to some extent that the patient cannot do anything about these meaningless things. It can be expected that the adverse effects of these behaviors on others, in turn, will have other consequences, such as creating a feeling of depression and widespread anxiety in the patient, and even creating the basis for the deterioration of personal relationships in the obsessive person. For this reason, family therapists have stated that sometimes obsessive-compulsive disorder is rooted in marital distress and discomfort, and actually replaces the obvious marital conflicts. Based on this hypothesis, therapists should pay attention to couple therapy in addition to individual therapy (Davison et al. 2004)

Obsessive compulsive disorder (OCD) usually begins in adolescence or adulthood and affects 1 in 200 children and adolescents. Thoughtful or practical obsessions cause obsessive-compulsive disorder or significant distress. These obsessions prevent the normal flow of childhood, academic performance, social activities or relationships with others. Obsessive thoughts may change with the age of the child and may change a lot. A younger child with obsessive-compulsive disorder may have long and chronic thoughts about harming themselves or a family member.

For example, the obsessive thought of an intruder and a thief entering through a door or window that is not locked by a child cause him obsessively check all the doors and windows in the house after his parents have fallen asleep to relieve his anxiety and relax. After the last check and lock, he may fear that he has accidentally unlocked a door or window and then have to obsessively check again and again. An older child or teenager with obsessive-compulsive disorder may fear getting sick from microbes, AIDS, or contaminated food. And in order to cope with his feelings, he may follow ritualistic and obsessive rituals and expand them (behavior or activity that is repeated).Sometimes intellectual obsession and compulsions combine each other; "If I stop checking or washing my hands, I'm afraid something bad will happen, so I can't not do it, even though it doesn't make sense." Researchers demonstrate that obsessive-compulsive disorder (OCD) is a brain disorder and appears in family members. Although it does not mean that if the parents have this disorder, the child will definitely show signs of obsession. Also, recent studies have shown that OCD may manifest or worsen after a streptococcal bacterial infection. Also, the child may manifest obsessive-compulsive disorder without any family history. Children and adolescents often feel ashamed and distressed about their OCD. Many of them fear that they may be crazy and are hesitant to talk about their thoughts and behavior with others. Good communication between parents and children can lead to increased understanding of OCD and help parents to support their child appropriately.

Most children with OCD can be effectively treated with a combination of psychotherapy (especially cognitive-behavioral techniques) and specific medications, such as selective serotonin reuptake inhibitors (SSRIs). Also, family support and education are important components for success in treatment. In cases where obsessive-compulsive disorder is related to streptococcal infection, antibiotic treatment can be effective. Seeking help from a child and adolescent psychiatrist is important both to better understand the complex problems caused by OCD and to treat obsessions American Academy of Child and Adolescent Psychiatry (AACAP), 2012).

Some consider the existence of obsessions in children far less than in adults, on the other hand, some believe that 50% or even most of the obsessions of adults started in childhood but were not diagnosed. It is rarely seen that children under 10 years old are taken to a psychiatrist because of obsession.

Obsessive state is usually more common in people with obsessive personality. These people are very organized, narrow-minded, thoughtful, conscientious, shy, and frank and love order. Because most obsessive children have obsessive parents and usually there is more than one affected person in the family of patients, therefore the issue of inheritance and genetics is considered an important factor. Of course, the role of educational factors should not be neglected because it plays a major role in the incidence and severity of the disease.

Perfectionist mothers, who have less flexibility, make the child learn and do all the things correctly and according to the principles from the very early age, and as a result, these behaviors are fixed and permanent in the child. The difference between obsessive-compulsive youth and children is that obsessive-compulsive youth do not need help from others to suppress their obsessive thoughts, while obsessive-compulsive children do not and regularly ask their mothers for help in dressing, make-up, and answering a series of questions. Of course, in all these cases, the mother must strictly implement the special and desired order of the child. In general, the mother should continuously pay attention to the obsessive needs of the child. Due to the inability of an inflexible mother to tolerate these conditions, the child may be punished and as a result the child's discomfort will increase.

Psychoanalysts consider obsession to be a replacement mechanism and they believe that the child resorts to the symptoms of obsession after facing failure. Obsessive thoughts are intrusive and unavoidable thoughts that originate from the person themselves and cause inconsistency and even abnormal behavior in children and adolescents as in adults. These behavioral disorders often make children and teenagers see a physician. If the child is older, he knows very well that these thoughts are illogical and meaningless, and he tries to somehow get rid of these disturbing thoughts, but no matter what he tries, his anxiety and worry increases, and because he cannot stop ruminating disturbing thoughts, reluctantly accepts them and engages himself in compulsive rituals behaviors. The contents of children's obsessions are different and thoughts such as why and how God was created or how man was created are seen in these children. Obsessions are often accompanied by compulsions. For example, a child should touch only one of several trees or light poles, or should not put his foot on the mosaic lines of the school yard, because it may be a danger to him or his family! The presence of the patient's resistance and persistence to get rid of the evil of disturbing thoughts and the awareness that these thoughts are not only absurd and meaningless, but also created by his own mind and not imposed on him from the outside are among the characteristics that lead to the diagnosis of obsession and schizophrenia.

The symptoms of obsession may manifest in different forms, including common symptoms such as restlessness, making excuses, insomnia and insomnia, anorexia, and psychosomatic complaints are common symptoms. These symptoms are often not recognized unless they are accompanied by severe neurotic symptoms or cause great incompatibility. Obsessive thoughts of children have mostly symbolic aspects that are created as a result of the intellectual conflict of children or adolescents. Arson may be seen in teenagers and children with obsessions. It means to burn the people who have taken the love and affection of their parents by lighting a fire. In other words, arson, considering its dangers, is a symbol of losing the love of parents or destroying one's rivals. Under the pressure of obsessive thoughts, teenagers may cut their eyebrows, eyelashes and facial hair (tricotillomania) and steal which is different from thefts of people with severe mental disorders. A distinction must be made between obsessive behavior and habits. In the habits, doing actions does not cause discomfort and anxiety, and there is no resistance to disturbing thoughts. With the explanations that were given, it is difficult to diagnose obsession in children and teenagers, and for this reason, the treatment starts very late and the disease progresses, and even after treatment, the possibility of the disease returning is very high. The first symptoms of the return of the disease are the reappearance of the child's incompatibilities. In order to treat obsession, long-term psychotherapy should be done along with pharmacotherapy. So far, it has not been seen that obsessive illness can be cured without the intervention of a psychiatrist. The child should be allowed to talk about his thoughts, even if they are absurd and meaningless, without feeling discomfort or criticism. Since most of these patients have not talked to anyone about their obsessions and mental conflicts before going to a psychiatrist. Most parents do not know about their child's obsessive thoughts, and even the child himself does not know that his thoughts are obsessive. Establishing correct and favorable communication between the doctor and the child is essential for treatment. The child should be able to express his neglected and displaced discomforts, which he has pretended as an obsession. Play therapy, painting, story writing, sculpting while venting and expressing the child's discomfort makes the patient realize the origin of his behavioral disorders.In addition, parents find out what their child's discomfort is and treat the child to get his satisfaction while eliminating deprivations and failures (Milani Far, 2019).

Symptoms of obsessive-compulsive disorder were identified in the 17th century. At the time, mental and practical obsessions were described as manifestations of religious melancholy, and people with obsessions were considered "possessed" by outside forces. In the first half of the 19th century, OCD was investigated as a scientific topic. In 1838, a French psychiatrist named Jean Dominique Esquirol first described obsession as a medical disorder almost similar to the description of contemporary obsessive-compulsive disorder and classified it as "monomania "(a type of minor delusion). At the end of the 19th century, OCD was classified as "mental fatigue" (neurasthenia). In the 20th century, Sigmund Freud and Pierre Janet, a French psychologist, separated OCD from neurasthenia (mental fatigue).In 1903, Pierre Janet proposed that obsessive patients have an abnormal personality (he called it " psychastenia" mental weakness) with features such as anxiety, great worry, and doubt, and explained the successful treatment of ritualistic and obsessive behavior using similar techniques like is used in behavioral therapy today. Janet reported a case of a five-year-old boy who suffered from mental weakness (psychastenia) with disturbing and repetitive thoughts. This was the first clinical description of obsessive-compulsive disorder in children. Currently, both the Diagnostic and Statistical Manual of Mental Disorders (DSM; American Psychiatric Association, 2000) and the International Classification of Diseases (ICD; World Health Organization, 1992) use the same diagnostic criteria for children, adolescents, and adults, with the difference that "insight" (relative to obsessive-compulsive disorder) is not necessary for children (Alvarenga et al., 2012).

Obsessive-compulsive disorder patients usually refer to spiritual authorities other than psychiatrists. Patients with obsessive thoughts and actions (both with obsessive thoughts and with obsessive actions) make up at least 75% of affected patients. Some researchers believe that if patients are evaluated precisely in terms of mental practical obsessions (mental actions) in addition to behavioral obsessions, this estimation may approach 100%. For example, an obsessive thought about harming a child may be followed by an obsessive mental act of repeating a certain prayer a certain number of times. However, some researchers and physicians believe that some patients only have obsessive thoughts and not obsessive actions. Such patients may have recurrent thoughts about a sexual act or aggression that is to blame for the patient himself. To facilitate, it is better to consider obsession as a thought and compulsion as a behavior. Obsessive thoughts and actions have common characteristics, an insistent and urgent thought or impulse enters the conscious mind of a person, a feeling of intense anxiety is associated with the main manifestation of the phenomenon and often leads to defensive measures against the initial thought or impulse, the obsessive thought or action is ego-dystonic. It is inescapable, that is, it is strange and alien to a person's experience of himself as a mental being. Regardless of the clarity and compulsion of obsessive thoughts and actions, a person is aware of their absurdity and illogicality, a person suffering from obsessive thoughts and actions feels a strong desire to resist them. However, almost half of patients show little resistance to their obsessive actions.

Almost 80% of patients consider their obsessive behavior irrational and stupid. Sometimes the obsessive thoughts and actions become extremely valuable to the patient, for example, patients may insist that compulsive grooming is morally right, even if they lose their jobs because of the time spent cleaning.

The manifestation of obsessive thoughts and actions in adults as well as children and adolescents is diverse and different. Each patient's symptoms may overlap or change over time, but obsessive-compulsive disorder has four main patterns:

- **Contamination**: The most common pattern of obsession is contamination followed by washing or forced avoidance of the supposedly contaminated object. The frightening object is often something that cannot be avoided (such as urine, feces, germs, and dust). Such patients may wash their hands excessively or be unable to leave the house due to fear of microbes. Although anxiety is the most common emotional response to a frightening object, shame and obsessive hatred are also common. Patients suffering from contamination obsession usually believe that contamination spreads from one object to another, from person to person with minor contact.
- **Morbid Doubt**: The second most common pattern of obsession is doubt followed by a compulsion to try. Obsessions usually involve danger or violence (like forgetting to turn off the faucet or lock the

door).Experimentation may require several trips back home and to the stove. Such patients have an obsessive lack of self-confidence and always feel guilty for forgetting or doing something.

— **Intrusive thoughts**: The third most common pattern of obsessive compulsive disorder is intrusive thoughts without obsessive actions. These obsessive thoughts are usually repetitive thoughts of some kind of sexual or aggressive act that the patient considers to be blameworthy.

— **Symmetry**: The fourth most common pattern is the need for symmetry and accuracy, which can lead to obsessive compulsiveness. Such patients may spend hours eating or grooming themselves.

In more than half of patients with obsessive-compulsive disorder, the onset of symptoms is acute. In about 50 to 70 percent of cases, the onset of symptoms occurs after a stressful event, such as pregnancy, sexual issues, or the death of a beloved one. Because many patients hide their symptoms, there is often a delay of 5 to 10 years in meeting a psychiatrist, and of course, this delay is decreasing as people become more aware. The course of the disorder is usually chronic.

In some patients, symptoms fluctuate and in others remain constant. About 20 to 30 percent of these patients have significant improvement, and 40 to 50 percent have moderate improvement. There are different reports that 20 to 40% of patients do not show any symptoms of recovery or their symptoms increase daily. Almost one third of these patients suffer from severe depression and suicide is an important risk in all these patients.

The darker prognosis has correlation with the comorbidity of major depressive disorder, delusional beliefs, the presence of overvalued beliefs (i.e. the acceptance of some obsessive actions and thoughts), the comorbidity of a personality disorder (especially schizotypal personality disorder), submission to obsessive actions (up to resistance to it), childhood onset, more unusual obsessive-compulsive behavior, and the need for hospitalization. A good prognosis is related to good occupational and social adjustment, the presence of a detector event, and the periodic nature of symptoms. Obsessive thought content apparently has nothing to do with prognosis (Sadock et al ,2007). At the end of this section, the diagnostic criteria of DSM-5 (American Psychiatric Association, 2013) for obsessive-compulsive disorder (OCD) are delivered:

A. Presence of mental obsessions, practical obsessions/ compulsions or both:

Obsessions are determined by items (1) and (2):

1- Repetitive and resistant thoughts, desires or mental images that are experienced during the disorder, disturbing and unwanted and cause anxiety or distress in most people.

2- The person tries to ignore these thoughts, desires, or mental images, prevent them from occurring, or neutralize them with another thought or action. (i.e. by doing an obsessive behavior/compulsion).

Practical obsessions/compulsions are determined by items (1) and (2):

1- Repetitive behaviors (eg, washing hands, tidying up, checking) or mental acts (eg, praying, counting, repeating words slowly) as the person feels compelled to do them in response to an obsessive or principled thought which must be accomplish carefully.

2- Behaviors or mental actions are designed to prevent or reduce anxiety or distress, or prevent a fearful situation or event. But these behaviors or mental actions have nothing to do with what they are supposed to prevent or neutralize or are clearly extreme.

Note: Young children may not be able to express the goals of these behaviors or mental actions.

B. Obsessions are time-consuming (e.g. take more than an hour per day) or cause clinically significant distress or interfere with social activities, job performance, or other important functional areas of life.

C. Obsessive-compulsive symptoms are not caused by the physiological effects of a substance (e.g. substance abuse, prescription drugs) or other medical conditions.

D. The disorder is not better explained by symptoms of another mental disorder (eg, excessive worry in generalized anxiety disorder, preoccupation with appearance in body dysmorphic disorder, difficulty disposing of or losing possessions in hoarding disorder, plucking hair in trichotillomania , Skin peeling in excoriation disorder, stereotypies in stereotypic movement disorder, ritualized eating behavior in eating disorders, Mental preoccupation with substances or gambling in substance – related and addictive disorders, Mental preoccupation with having a disease in illness anxiety disorder, Fantasy or sexual desires in paraphilic disorders (paraphilia), impulses in disruptive disorders , impulse – control and conduct disorders, ruminations or feel guilty in major depressive disorder, delusional preoccupations in schizophrenia spectrum and other psychotic disorders or repetitive behavior patterns in autism spectrum disorder.

✧ **Specify if:**

- **With good or fairly good insight**: the person recognizes that the beliefs held in OCD are definitely or probably not true, or that they may be true or false.

- **With poor insight**: the person thinks that the beliefs held in obsessive-compulsive disorder are probably true.

- **No Insight / Delusional Beliefs**: The person strongly believes that the beliefs present in obsessive-compulsive disorder are true.

✧ **Specify** if:

- **Tic-related**: The individual has a past or current history of a tic disorder (American Psychiatric Association, 2013).

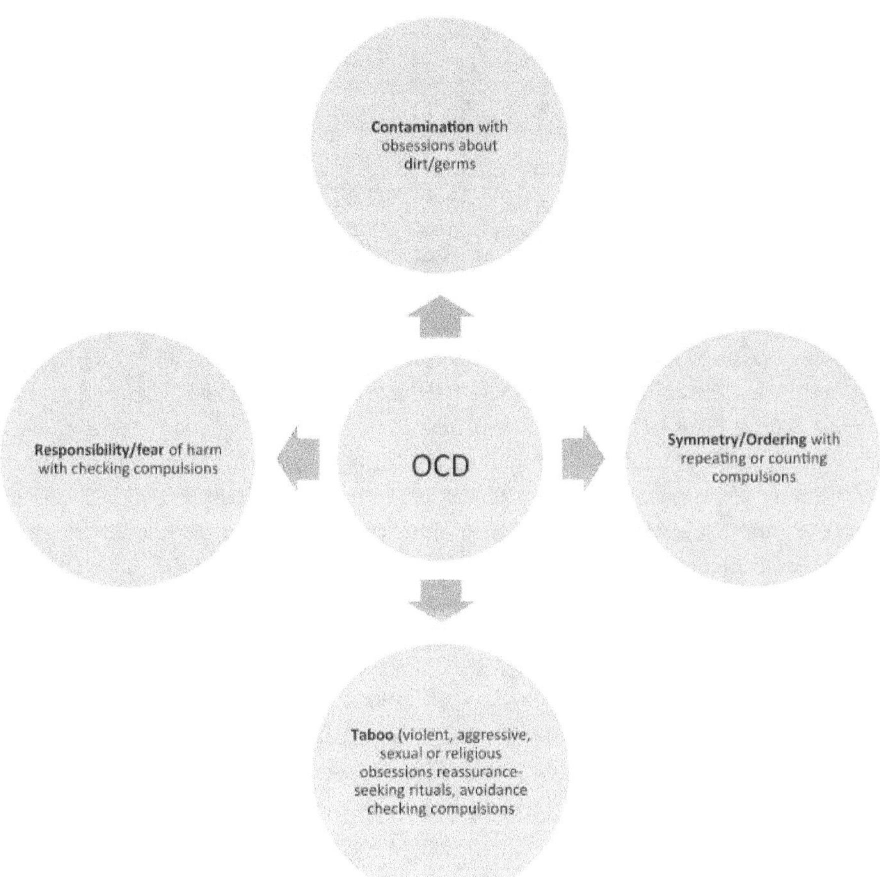

Fig. 1. OCD symptom sub-types. OCD symptoms are classically defined by four subtypes, including (1) responsibility/fear of harm (obsessions regarding responsibility and checking compulsions such as asking for reassurance or checking that harm did not occur to someone), (2) contamination (obsessions about dirt or germs or other possible contaminants and cleaning compulsions), (3) symmetry/ordering (obsessions about symmetry or order and ordering, repeating or counting compulsions), and (4) taboo (violent, aggressive, sexual or religious obsessions with reassurance-reeking rituals, avoidance or checking for harm).(Strom, N.I. et al,2021).

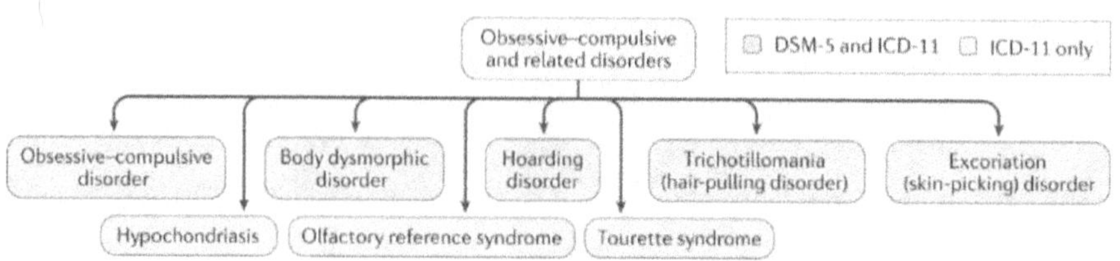

Fig. 2. Obsessive–compulsive and related disorders. The obsessive–compulsive and related disorders (OCRDs) chapter in the Diagnostic and Statistical Manual of Mental Disorders, Fifth Edition (DSM-5) includes obsessive–compulsive disorder (OCD; previously classified as an anxiety disorder), body dysmorphic disorder (previously classified as a somatoform disorder) and trichotillomania (previously classified as an impulse control disorder), as well as hoarding disorder and excoriation (skin-picking) disorder (both of which are new to the classification system). In the International Classification of Diseases, 11th Revision (ICD-11), this chapter also includes Tourette syndrome (also classified as a neurodevelopmental disorder), hypochondriasis (also classified as an anxiety disorder) and olfactory reference syndrome (which is new to the classification system). Similar to OCD, the OCRDs are often prevalent but under-recognized conditions that are characterized by repetitive and unwanted thoughts or behaviours. Some OCRDs include preoccupations and compulsive behaviours (such as body dysmorphic disorder), but others have predominantly motoric or behavioural symptoms (such as trichotillomania). Sensory phenomena, including premonitory urges and 'just right' perceptions (where a patient continues their compulsions until there is a feeling that things are 'just right' and they can stop), can be present in some OCRDs, including OCD and Tourette syndrome. (Stein ,D.J. et al, 2020).

2. EPIDEMIOLOGY OF OBSESSIVE COMPULSIVE DISORDER

Estimates of the prevalence and occurrence of OCD have been investigated in many studies in recent years. The first attempts to estimate the prevalence of OCD date back to the early 1950s, when Rudin stated that 0.05% of the general population suffers from this disorder. In more than the next two decades, studies showed that this disorder is relatively rare (Krochmalik & Menzies, 2003).

It should be noted that these studies were conducted on a percentage of patients who were hospitalized for treatment and did not include all diagnostic criteria of OCD. In the 1980s, the use of semi-structured interviews in studies to estimate the prevalence of OCD became popular. The Epidemiological Catchment Area (ECA) program was conducted in the early 1980s in an attempt to investigate the epidemiology of common psychopathology in 5 communities in the United States. The goals of this research project were: to determine the lifetime and 6-month prevalence of OCD in the general population with a random survey of more than 30,000 people and to investigate where patients with OCD look for treatment. (Rasmussen & Eisen1992). Amateur interviewers were trained to implement the Diagnostic Interview Schedule (DIS) based on DSM-III (Diagnostic and Statistical Manual of Mental Disorders) diagnostic criteria.

The results of the Epidemiological Catchment Area Study (ECA) showed that the prevalence of OCD is higher than the values that were shown in the initial reports. But the most interesting finding was that the lifetime prevalence of OCD ranges from 1.9% to 3.3%. (Krochmalik & Menzies, 2003) a finding that was 70-40 times closer to today's findings. Also, the findings showed that OCD is twice as common as schizophrenia or panic disorder. In fact, OCD was diagnosed as the fourth most common psychiatric disorder in the population of the United States of America (Pigott, 1998). Another epidemiologic study was conducted on 3258 citizens living in Edmonton, Canada, who were randomly selected using the same tools and detection method used in the study (ECA).

The results of this research also confirmed the findings of the study (ECA) in the United States of America. Bland et al. (1988) found that the lifetime prevalence of OCD in a Canadian sample is 3%, which was in line with the results of the (ECA) study(Krochmalik & Menzies, 2003).

These findings made a significant change in the estimation of the prevalence of OCD. Therefore, it was important to determine whether these findings are replicable, especially across different cultures.

The International OCD Study Group (CNCG- The Cross-National OCD Collaborative Group study) (Weissman et al.,1994) evaluated and compared the prevalence of OCD in six countries: Canada, Germany, Korea, New Zealand, Puerto Rico, and Taiwan. The results of this study were comparable to the findings of the prevalence of OCD in the Epidemiological Catchment Area (ECA) in the United States of America. Taiwan was the only country that showed a significantly lower prevalence of OCD. But it is interesting to note that this finding in Taiwan is in line with the low prevalence of other psychiatric disorders reported in the same study in Taiwan. (Pigott 1998).Why do the results of these large-scale epidemiological studies show a much higher prevalence of OCD compared to initial reports? Some of the reasons for this difference are as follows: firstly, as mentioned earlier, the initial estimates were based only on clinical judgments without the use of diagnostic tools to estimate the prevalence. Given the low level of knowledge and awareness about OCD at the time (the time of the original studies), it is not surprising that clinicians typically did not consider OCD diagnostic criteria when evaluating their patients. Generally, due to the low social understanding of this disorder in the past (and the potential high social shame that existed towards OCD), many people may have avoided expressing their disorder to others. Accordingly, the number of people who were considered with this disorder was underestimated. Additionally, it should be considered that until recently, OCD was considered a purely medical disorder and was generally treated within a medication-based framework. There is no doubt that at least some people with OCD sought help from relatives, friends, healers, priests, and clergy, and did not seek drug-based help from physicians.

These reasons have caused the number of patients to decrease and affect the initial estimates of the prevalence rate. Of course, it is possible that as early studies reported low numbers of people suffering from OCD, contemporary studies may have resulted in over-diagnosis of OCD. Given the level of interest and attention (researchers) to OCD, the number of treatments available for this disorder, and the attention of the public media, contemporary reports of the prevalence rate may have been biased toward a tendency to overestimate. Clinicians may overdiagnose this disorder, at least in part. Since, nowadays, they are most likely to self-diagnose this disorder. In general, considering the difficulties that currently exist in differential diagnosis and the misclassification of other disorders as OCD; it is possible that today's estimates are an exaggeration of the true prevalence of

OCD.

The lifetime prevalence of obsessive-compulsive disorder in the general population is estimated at 2-3%. Some researchers have estimated that the prevalence of this disorder is up to 10% among outpatients of psychiatric clinics. These figures place obsessive-compulsive disorder in the fourth row of the most common psychiatric diagnoses after the group of phobias, substance-related disorders, and depressive disorders. Epidemiological studies in Europe, Asia and Africa have confirmed these correlations across cultural boundaries. Among adults, men and women are equally likely to be affected, however, among teenagers; boys are more likely to be affected by obsessive-compulsive disorder than girls.

The average age of onset of this disorder is around 20 years old. Although in men, the starting age is a little lower (about 19 years old) than in women (about 22 years old). Overall, symptoms begin before age 25 in approximately two-thirds of patients, and symptoms begin after age 35 in less than 15% of cases. OCD may begin in adolescence or childhood, and in some cases as young as 2 years old.

Single people are more likely to be diagnosed with OCD than married people, although this finding probably reflects the difficulty of OCD patients in maintaining relationships. Obsessive-compulsive disorder is less common among black people than among white people, although differences in access to health care may account for much of this difference, rather than differences in prevalence between races (Sadock et al ,2007).

Researchers show that about 1% of teenagers have OCD. Estimates of the prevalence of this disorder in adolescents in different countries have been reported between 0.1% and 4% of the population (Heyman et al., 2001). There are no studies that have examined the prevalence of this disorder in teenagers on an annual basis, and most of the studies have been conducted on children at an advanced age and not on children at pre- puberty ages. However, Heyman et al. (2001) reported a steady increase in the number of cases in the age range of 5 to 15 years. Differences in diagnostic criteria and survey methods (such as differences in interview methods and whether interviews were conducted by professional or amateur clinicians) and motivation to participate in the study (for example, one of the high estimates was in a sample of Israeli adolescent soldiers) may be some probable causes of diversity and dispersion in OCD prevalence estimates. In the studies conducted by Flament et al. (1988) and Heyman et al. (2001) showed that this disease was not diagnosed by clinical services in most adolescents and therefore, they did not receive treatment (Williams & Waite, 2009). Generally, OCD begins in two periods of life, one near puberty and the other in early adulthood (Pauls et al., 1995). Probably, the onset of OCD is increasing in this era due to the developmental transitions towards independent lifestyles. Although very rare cases of children aged 3 or 4 with OCD have also been reported. OCD usually appears gradually. But it may appear suddenly, often in response to a traumatic life event (Lensi et al., 1996) McKeon et al. (1984) found that individuals with OCD experienced significantly more traumatic life events than the control group in the 12 months prior to the onset of the obsession. According to our clinical experience, OCD in teenagers often appears after conflicts, problems with friends and the illness or death of a family member. Thomsen (1999) has described parental divorce and marital discord, as well as experiences such as illness and accidents, as factors contributing to the development of OCD (Williams & Waite, 2009). Studies show that the appearance of OCD in boys is twice as high as in girls before puberty. (Geller et al., 1998; Rasmussen and Eisen, 1992; Zohar, 1999).But in adulthood, this disorder is seen in equal proportion in men and womenalthough there are differences in the type of obsessive symptoms of men and women, for example women are more afraid of contamination and are obsessed with washing and cleaning, but men are more likely to experience obsessional slowness or sexual obsessions. It has been observed that only about half of adolescents with OCD seek help and treatment.The reasons for the lack of importance to treatment and asking for help can include the following: lack of awareness or understanding of the problem (lack of awareness of family members or the teenager himself); fear that if the concern about the obsessive thoughts is expressed, the likelihood of happening the obsessive thoughts (or coming true) will increase; Shame, fear of what others will think of them or how they will treat them, and what will happen if they ask professional help and treatment. Many people with OCD report intense feelings of shame and humiliation due to their obsessive thoughts. They may often know that checking or washing won't actually change anything, but feel powerless to stop their obsessive thoughts. As a result, these people may be less likely to ask help (Williams & Waite, 2009).

More importantly, when these individuals ask help they may not initially disclose information about OCD (Torres et al., 2007). This state may be due to being ashamed and embarrassed about describing their obsessive symptoms or due to not asking the right questions on the part of professionals. Stobie et al. (2007) found that adults with OCD were diagnosed an average of eight and a half years after the onset of obsessive-compulsive symptoms that significantly interfered with their lives.

Raj was a 13-year-old boy who described seeing his younger sister in the bathroom and being sexually aroused. After this incident, he felt that he might be a paedophile and especially that he might sexually abuse his sister. As a result, he tried hard to get these thoughts out of his mind and prayed that he would be strong enough to control himself. Because he felt like he was about to act out those thoughts, he avoided being alone with her sister. He saw himself as Satan and was deeply ashamed of his thoughts. Although his family had noticed his increasing depression and isolation, they were unsure of its cause. He was unable to talk about his thoughts with his family members because he believed that if he told them his thoughts, they would hate him and not love him anymore (Williams & Waite, 2009).

Epidemiological studies in Europe, Asia, and Africa have shown a relatively high prevalence of this disorder in different cultures, and despite the differences in the content of obsessive symptoms, their form has undeniable similarities. Cultural variables can affect the manifestations of obsessive-compulsive disorder. For example, Steketee believes that religion as a cultural phenomenon can play the role of a mediator in obsessive-compulsive disorder (Dadfar et al, 2001; Salehi et al., 2004). Qasemzadeh et al. (2002) investigated OCD symptoms with "Modsley Scale" in a sample of Iranian patients, and the results showed that doubt and indecision is the most common mental obsession and washing is the most common practical obsession in the entire sample. Fear of dirt and pollution and obsessive thoughts about being dirty and obsession with washing were more common in women, while blasphemous thoughts and obsessions with order were more common in men. In a study on the phenomenology of OCD in Egypt, it was shown that the most common mental obsessions are religious and pollution (60%) and physical (49%) and the most common compulsions are repetitive obsessive rituals (68%), cleaning and washing (63%) and checking (58%).In addition, the results indicate that one third of the patients also suffered from depression and the educational role of religion in the phenomenology of OCD in Egypt has been raised. Tezcan & Millet (1997) investigated the phenomenology of this disorder in eastern Turkey in their research. The results of this study demonstrated that the fear of dirt and pollution, followed by religious obsessions, were the most common obsessions. Egrilmez, Gulseren & Kultur (1997) in their study on the phenomenology of obsessions in Turkish patients with OCD concluded that depressive disorder is the most important comorbidity in 73% of patients and the most common obsessions are related to daily activities (64%) and pollution fields (53%). They believed that Islamic culture has not had a significant effect on the phenomenology of this disorder.Thomsen (1997) investigated obsessive-compulsive symptoms in Danish children and adolescents and concluded that thoughts about dirt and pollution are the most common obsessive content and the phenomenological composition is similar in girls and boys with very little difference. No cross-cultural differences were observed in the content of obsessive thoughts and compulsive behavior of Danish, Indian and Japanese children and adolescents. Lensi et al. concluded in their research that men often have symptoms such as obsessions with symmetry, sex, accuracy, and unusual rituals, and women have more aggressive obsessions. Akhtar, Wig, Varma, Pershad & Verma (1978) showed in their study that the form of mental and practical obsessions is influenced by internal factors (age, gender, and intelligence) and their content, at least similarly, by external factors (Religion, geographic location and social class) (Salehi et al, 2004).

Although the concept of obsession was proposed years ago, the criteria for diagnosing OCD were completed and modified in recent years' research, which can be partially attributed to the fact that OCD generally occurs in the context of other disorders.

OCD is a common psychiatric disorder that usually begins in adolescence. Although the initial findings declared the prevalence of obsessive compulsive disorder in the general population at 0.5% regional epidemiologic studies showed its prevalence in lifetime reported 2.5% (one out of every 40 people) and its prevalence in six months was 1.6%.

Most studies conducted on large general populations have defined nonclinical OCD very similarly to OCD. The prevalence of OCD in the Iranian population is estimated at 1.8% (0.7% in men and 2.8% in women). Obsession affects men and women almost equally.

Studies on the relationship between socio-economic status and obsession have different results. A study in England showed that most children with obsessions are from families with low socio-economic status.

If the study of Diler & Avci (2002) stated that most of the children and teenagers with obsessions in Turkey were from the middle and upper classes Valleni-Basile et al. (1994) in a survey of 3283 seventh and eighth grade teenagers determined the cross-sectional prevalence of "non-clinical obsession" in this population at 19%. In addition, Maina et al. (1999) also concluded that OC syndrome is common in the healthy adolescent population, and as a result, the presence of OC symptoms in adolescents can be considered a natural phenomenon.

The study of Humaida, et al (2004) estimated the prevalence of obsession in Egyptian students at 9.1%. Degonda, Wyss & Angst (1993) and Ismail (1998) also reported it as 5.5 and 8.4 percent, respectively. Although Zohar (1999) and Stein, Forde, Anderson & Walker (1997) found the prevalence of obsession lower than what they predicted (0.6 percent), but in the study of Maina et al. (1999), the lifetime prevalence of obsessive symptoms was estimated at 12.3%. The diagnostic boundary of OCD is not always easy and people may show different results at different times, and this can be a justification for observing diverse results of studies. Valleni-Basile et al. (1994) also estimated the rate of clinical obsession at 0.7% and non-clinical obsession at 8.4% in a study investigating the epidemiology of obsessions among teenagers. In his opinion, estimating the mentioned percent is a normal thing in a healthy population, especially teenagers. It is necessary to carry out wider investigations in different regions of the world to obtain a more coherent and comprehensive result (Brynska, 1997, Shams et al., 2007). The recent findings in the field of widespread prevalence of obsessive-compulsive symptoms in the non-clinical community and the lack of distinction between the concept and the form of obsessions in obsessive and healthy people are a new achievement in the field of theoretical discussions of OCD. It seems that the difference between obsessive-compulsive disorder in clinical and non-clinical society is not in its "content" but in its "severity".Brynska (1997) believes that the ratio of prevalence of obsession with the age of onset of the disease is different in women and men, in such a way that men are diagnosed with this disorder earlier than women, but the number of women who are diagnosed during adolescence are more than men.

In some studies, the difference in the prevalence of obsession in women and men has been confirmed (Shams et al., 2007). In studies on children and adolescents, the ratio of the prevalence of this disorder in men to women has been estimated as three to two (Geller et al., 1998), while the amount of obsessive-compulsive symptoms in adult men and women is equal (Antony et al., 1998). In Ismail's study (1998) the prevalence of obsession was higher in women than in men. The findings show that the prevalence of OCD in the Iranian population is higher in women than in men (Mohammadi et al., 2005). According to Humaida et al. (2004), perhaps the reason for the difference in prevalence between third world countries and developed countries can be found in cultural differences and the type and amount of responsibility of men in the third world(Shams et al., 2007).

According to the American Psychiatric Association (APA, 2013), the 12-month prevalence of OCD in the United States is 1.2%. The prevalence rate is similar to the international prevalence (1.1 to 1.8 percent), in adulthood, women suffer from this disorder at a somewhat higher rate than men. Although men are usually more affected by this disorder in childhood, in the United States, the average age of onset of OCD is 19.5 years, and in 25% of cases, it starts at the age of 14. Onset of OCD after the age of 35 is uncommon, but is possible. Men are diagnosed with this disorder at a younger age than women. The onset of OCD occurs before the age of 10 in approximately 25% of males.

The onset of symptoms is usually gradual. However, sudden onset has also been reported. If OCD is not treated, the process of the disease usually becomes chronic and the symptoms gradually increase. In some people, the course of the disease is mild and implicit, but in a small number of people, the course of the disease worsens.

The recovery rate without treatment is low in adults (only 20% of people reevaluated 40 years later). The onset of the disorder in childhood or adolescence may cause lifelong OCD. However, 40 percent of people who develop OCD in childhood or adolescence may recover by early adulthood. The course of OCD disease is often complicated by the occurrence of other disorders along with this disease. Compulsions in children are easier to diagnose than Obsessive thoughts because compulsions are visible, but most children have both of them (as do most adults). The pattern of OCD symptoms in adults can be stable over time, but it changes more in children. Differences in the theme and content of mental obsessions and practical obsessions have been reported in the samples of children and adolescents compared to the samples of adults. These differences are probably a reflection of the relevant characteristics of different stages of transformation (for example, a higher rate of sexual and religious obsessions in adolescents compared to children); a higher rate of obsessions related to being harmed in children and adolescents than in adults (for example, fears related to painful events such as death or illness of oneself or beloved ones) (American Psychiatric Association, 2013).

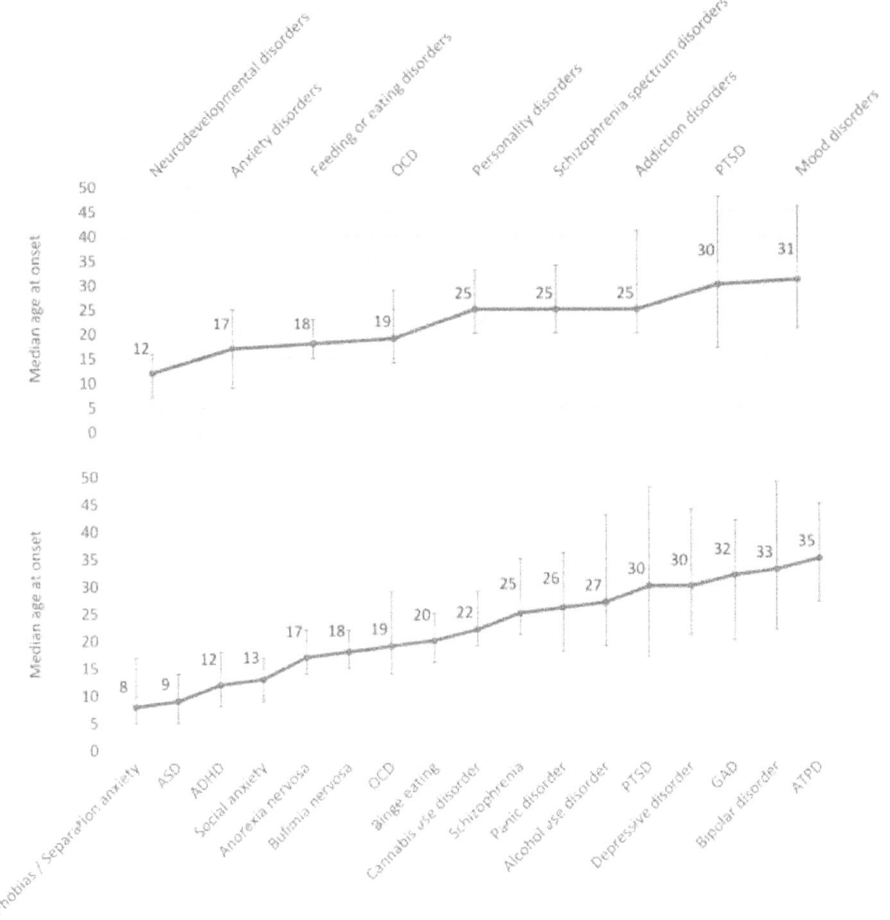

Fig. 1. Meta-analytic median age at onset of mental disorders. The line indicates the median age at onset of mental disorders (ICD-11 diagnostic blocks or spectra above, specific mental disorders below), the bar indicates the 25th and 75th percentiles. ICD-11 blocks of mental disorders. Addiction disorders: disorders due to substance use or addictive behaviour, Anxiety and fear: anxiety and fear-related disorders, OCD related: obsessive-compulsive or related disorders, Schizophrenia spectrum disorders: schizophrenia-spectrum and primary psychotic disorders. ICD-11 specific mental disorders. ADHD attention deficit hyperactivity disorder, ASD: autism spectrum disorder, ATPD, acute and transient psychotic disorder; Binge eating: binge eating disorder, Bipolar disorder: bipolar or related disorders, GAD generalised anxiety disorder, OCD obsessive-compulsive disorder, Phobia: specific phobia, PTSD post-traumatic stress disorder, Separation anxiety: separation anxiety disorder, Social anxiety: social anxiety disorder. (Solmi , M. et al, 2022).

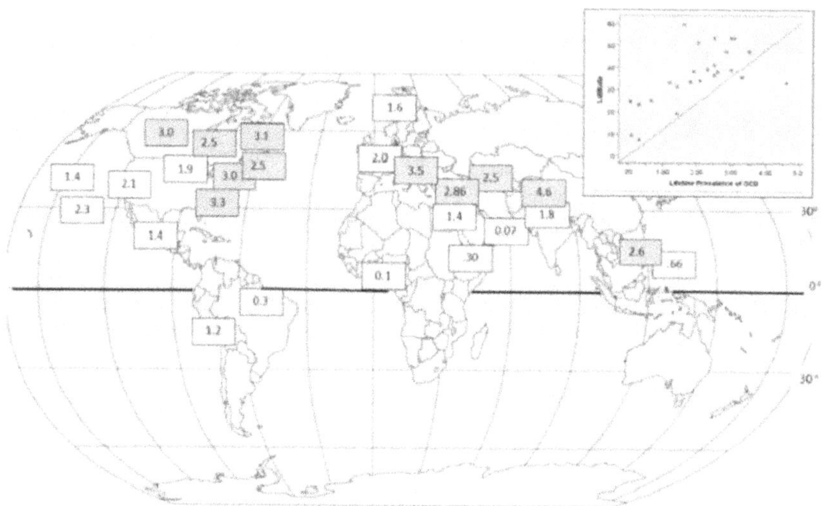

Fig. 2. World map including estimates of the prevalence of OCD. Graph in upper right show the correlation between latitude and lifetime OCD rates. (Coles, M.E. et al, 2018). Note: White = prevalence < 2.5 , Shading = prevalence > 2.5

3. COMORBIDITY OF OCD
WITH OTHER DISORDERS

An individual with OCD usually suffers from other mental disorders as well. The prevalence of the major depressive disorder in OCD is about 67% and for social phobia is 25%. Common psychiatric diagnoses of OCD include alcohol abuse disorder, generalized anxiety disorder, specific phobia, panic disorder, eating disorders, and personality disorders. The incidence rate of Tourette's disorder in OCD is 5-7%, and 20-30% of individuals with OCD have a history of tics. Major neurological disorders that should be considered in the differential diagnosis include Tourette's disorder, other tic disorders, temporal lobe epilepsy, and rarely trauma and post-encephalitis. The characteristic symptoms of Tourette's disorder are motor and vocal tics that occur frequently and almost every day. Tourette's disorder and obsessive-compulsive disorder have the same age of onset and similar symptoms. Major psychiatric considerations in the differential diagnosis of the obsessive-compulsive disorder include schizophrenia, obsessive-compulsive personality disorder, phobias, and depressive disorders.

Obsessive-compulsive disorder can usually be distinguished from this disease by the absence of other schizophrenic symptoms, less proximity of symptoms, and the patient's insight into his symptoms. An obsessive-compulsive personality disorder is not associated with functional impairment similar to obsessive-compulsive disorder. Phobias can be recognized by the lack of a relationship between obsession and compulsion. The major depressive disorder may sometimes be associated with obsessive thoughts, but patients who only suffer from obsessive-compulsive disorder do not meet the diagnostic criteria of major depressive disorder. Other mental disorders that may have a close relationship with the obsessive-compulsive disorder include hypochondriasis, body dysmorphic disorder, and possibly other impulse control disorders, such as obsessive-compulsive disorder and pathological gambling. All of these disorders involve either repetitive thoughts (e.g., worrying about one's body) or repetitive behavior (e.g., stealing). Compulsive sexual behavior may be related to OCD (Sadock et al ,2007).

OCD is only one of the reasons why children repeat a series of actions due to having it. Children under the age of 10 often have fixed repetitive rituals when sleeping. For example, children at this age may insist that their parents kiss them in a certain way before turning off the bedroom lights, or they have a special soft doll next to them. Although young children are unlikely to give a clear reason for their rituals and repetitive actions, older children may say that these dolls or rituals prevent monsters or other scary things from appearing. The reason for children's games may also include reasons similar to those seen in OCD. For example, when children walk alone, they may sing: "Don't step on the cracks because the devil will catch you."Certainly, in these cases, the fear is usually imaginary and not real. The key point in understanding and considering behavior as OCD is the degree of inefficiency and the impact of repetitive actions and obsessive rituals in daily life.

Another area of difficulty for clinicians is distinguishing OCD from stereotyped behaviors in children with learning disabilities or autism spectrum disorders. These children may repeat actions for other reasons, such as the immediate pleasure of doing something right or to reduce fatigue, and not because of the feeling of preventing harm (as in OCD). In these cases, these rituals have no meaning, but an individual with the autism spectrum may have OCD, so to determine the motivation of the behavior, a detailed description of mental experiences is necessary.

A 13-year-old boy with Asperger's syndrome had a ritual of counting before opening doors. When asked about his behavior, he explained that he felt something bad would happen if he didn't open the door at the right time. He could not express how many times he performed his particular ritual, but he could express anxiety or worried thoughts that arose before counting. He had other rituals, such as wearing clothes in a certain way, and he considered these rituals to be correct. Under a series of training, he was able to change these obsessive rituals because these rituals did not cause him distress. In this case, the reason for the diagnosis of OCD was that he felt that he had to do the counting ritual to prevent harm. While apparently, his special ritual of dressing was due to the fact that he preferred to do things in a certain order.

Children with OCD often have other psychological problems, with about 75% meeting full diagnostic criteria for a disorder (March et al., 2004; Williams and Waite, 2009).

It is not uncommon for many disorders to have a high rate of co-morbidity. A high rate of anxiety and depression occurs in OCD, but when anxiety or depression is the main problem, OCD is less likely to co-morbidity with these disorders (Shear et al., 2006). Other anxiety disorders such as generalized anxiety (anxiety that is not related to OCD and may be related to school, friendships, family, and life issues), separation anxiety (usually caused by separation from parents), and social anxiety (anxiety in the case of social situations) is common in OCD. A recent study of children's mental health in England showed that 52% of children with OCD also have an anxiety disorder co-occurring with OCD. There is considerable overlap in the phenomenology of cognition in OCD and anxiety, and they may be considered intrusive, structurally similar, recurrent, and persistent (Comer et al.,2004). Therefore, it is not clear whether these combined disorders indicate problems in the diagnostic system or multiple injuries? However, treating OCD through cognitive-behavior therapy (CBT) has a positive effect on other anxiety disorders as well (O'Kearney et al., 2006). Comorbidity of depression or dysthymia in children with OCD is not uncommon; studies have shown that more than 20% of children with OCD also have a mood disorder.

As much as OCD has a significant impact on children's lives, co-morbidity disorders often cause secondary problems for these children. While mild or moderate depression does not appear to have a significant effect on treatment response, severe depression is correlated with poorer treatment response (Abramowitz and Foa, 2000). Children with OCD also may experience externalizing disorders such as attention deficit hyperactivity disorder (ADHD), conduct disorder, or oppositional defiant disorder. Different studies have reported different levels of co-morbidity (other disorders with OCD) ranging from 10% to 44% (Thomsen, 1999).

This is probably due to the affected populations and how the behavior is classified. Many children are in conflict with their parents due to having OCD, and this conflict causes problems in diagnosis. Because the conflict may be due to children's obsessive-compulsive disorder, or it may be a separate issue that indicates a deeper problem, such as oppositional defiant disorder. Also, ADHD is found in clinical populations (suffering from obsessions) and may cause special problems for psychological treatment.

Careful planning may be necessary to maximize interventions and reduce the effects of impulsivity and attention deficit disorders. Children or their families often worry that their obsessions are a sign of insanity, but delusions do not arise from obsessive thoughts, and there is also no association between OCD and psychotic disorders (Salkovskis, 1996). An individual with OCD generally have insight into their disorder and recognize the irrationality of their behavior, while an individual with psychosis often lacks insight (into their illness). There is evidence that tic disorders are associated with OCD. Approximately 50% of children with Tourette syndrome (TS) have obsessive-compulsive behaviors, and higher rates of OCD have been observed in the immediate family of individuals with Tourette syndrome (TS) (Pauls et al., 1995). However, it is uncommon for tic disorders to develop after OCD. Compulsion in Tourette syndrome (TS) mostly includes touching, slow strokes, rubbing, blinking, and staring rituals, and less compulsion of order, cleaning, and washing are seen in this disorder (Hanna et al., 2002).

Compulsions may appear as a secondary problem; for example, when these individuals anticipate the occurrence of tics, they may become anxious and perform rituals to reduce their anxiety (Williams and Waite, 2009).

Usually, individuals with obsessive-compulsive disorder seek treatment while suffering from other symptoms and disorders such as depression, phobias, anxiety, and worry Anxiety disorders such as social phobia, specific phobias, and panic disorder are among the most common additional diagnoses; about 76% of obsessive-compulsive patients have diagnostic criteria for these anxiety disorders.Weissman et al (1994) found in their work that almost half of the Individuals with a current diagnosis of obsession also have the diagnostic criteria of another anxiety disorder. Mood disorders are also common in individuals with obsessive-compulsive disorder. The lifetime prevalence of any mood disorder is 60%, and the most common of them is major depressive disorder (41%).In other studies, it was found that approximately 30% of patients with a current diagnosis of obsessive-compulsive disorder also have diagnostic criteria for major depression. This matter is especially important from the point of view that according to the findings of some researches, severe depression will reduce the therapeutic effects of the cognitive behavioral approach.

The association between obsessions and eating disorders has also been reported in the research literature. About 10% of women with obsessive-compulsive disorder also reported a history of anorexia nervosa and 33% of women diagnosed with bulimia nervosa had a history of obsessive-compulsive disorder. Tic disorders also appear to be associated with obsessions. About 20 to 30% of individuals with obsessive-compulsive disorder have reported a current or past history of tics. Estimates of comorbidity of Tourette tic and obsessive-compulsive disorder range from 35 to 50% (Foa et al.,2012).

It is well established that patients with OCD generally have other psychiatric disorders as well. Epidemiological Catchment Area (ECA) study reported that two-thirds of patients with OCD show criteria for another psychiatric disorder in their lives.

Other studies have also shown a similar prevalence rate (Tükel et al., 2002; Hudak, 2011). In a study conducted in a specialized OCD treatment center, 31% of patients with OCD met the diagnostic criteria of major depressive disorder (MDD) during the period of their treatment at the center, and 67% of the study participants also showed a lifetime history of major depressive disorder (MDD). In total, the prevalence of clinical criteria (other disorders) that obsessive-compulsive patients showed at some stage of their lives was reported as follows: 18% of social phobia, 17% of eating disorders, 14% of alcohol dependence, and 12% of panic disorder, the prevalence of these diagnoses was 11%, 8%, 8%, and 6%, respectively (Attiullah et al., 2000)

Depression may be considered a secondary diagnosis, and as a result, OCD symptoms may be considered the main and primary diagnosis. Distinguishing between these two modes can be difficult. Nevertheless, the finding that major depressive disorder (MDD) is present in approximately two-thirds of OCD patients is an important issue for clinicians. Because major depressive disorder (MDD) is one of the diseases associated with suicide, there is a potential possibility of suicide in patients with OCD. Unfortunately, little research has been conducted on suicidality in OCD. A study reported that 70% of individuals with OCD have thoughts that life is worthless, about half of them have suicidal thoughts or wish to die, and 10% have a history of suicide attempts (Torres et al., 2007). The rate of suicide attempts in patients with OCD was reported to be 27% by other researchers (Kamath et al., 2007).

While these reports suggest that suicide is a potential topic of interest for OCD clinicians, OCD's unique risk factors for suicide are not yet well defined. Due to conflicting reports, it has not been determined whether there is a relationship between the severity of OCD symptoms and suicide. More studies are needed to clarify this issue. A type of OCD symptoms with the obsessive-compulsive disorder has been assumed as a risk factor (for suicide). But there has not been enough research in this regard yet. The presence of depression and hopelessness is associated with a higher degree of suicidal ideation (Kamath et al., 2007). Although insight into obsessive-compulsive symptoms is less clearly related to suicidal ideation, it has been observed that suicide is potentially present in OCD, and this issue should be investigated widely. It has been revealed that bipolar disorder comorbid with OCD. Several researchers have reported that one-third of patients with bipolar disorder also show OCD diagnostic criteria. It is worth mentioning that the symptoms of obsession and compulsion rarely occur during the manic period (Attiullah et al., 2000). Most patients with bipolar disorder and OCD report that when they are in a manic period, their obsession and compulsion symptoms decrease. Gordon and Rasmussen (1988) reported the exacerbation of the patient's obsessive-compulsive disorder was directly related to the depressive episode and decreased during the mania episodes. This is a fairly common clinical pattern. It is not uncommon for bipolar patients to report this phenomenon as a motivating factor for not using mood stabilizers (stereotyped behaviors). In general, due to the euphoria associated with manic episodes, these individual enjoy their lack of intellectual compulsions.

As mentioned, other anxiety disorders are generally comorbid with OCD, and the diagnosis of a generalized anxiety disorder (GAD) is often increasing in patients with OCD. About 20% of patients with obsessive-compulsive disorder have a generalized anxiety disorder (GAD) with obsessions (Abramowitz and Foa, 1998). The clinical distinction between obsessions and worries in generalized anxiety disorder (GAD) may be difficult in individuals who have clinical features of both disorders. Intense mental preoccupation with worrying about things that are potentially unlikely to happen is often seen in both diseases, and therefore the high comorbidity of these two disorders is generally not unexpected. As mentioned, approximately 17% of patients with OCD also have eating disorders, and 41% of patients with eating disorders may also have OCD (Kaye et al., 2004) which shows that these two disorders have some similar clinical features. Patients with eating disorders may show perfectionism, and inflexibility, especially in matters related to their eating habits and harm avoidance (Attiullah et al., 2000). These symptoms can increase in a person who suffers from both diseases (obsessive-compulsive disorder and eating disorder).

It should be kept in mind that a common obsession is the fear of contaminated food. An individual with this obsession often experiences weight loss. Because eating disorders are potentially fatal, such pathology does not guarantee an eating disorder diagnosis. In order to screen and diagnose eating disorders, examining patients with OCD is necessary. The linkage between tic disorders and OCD has long been known. It has been determined that between 5 - 10% of patients with OCD show the diagnostic criteria of Tourette syndrome, and up to 20% show multiple tics at some stage of their life (Hudak, 2011). Patients with Tourette syndrome are more likely to show OCD symptoms related to symmetry and order and obsessive touching and counting behaviors (Hasler et al., 2005). Almost a quarter of patients with tic disorders have OCD, and more than half of them report obsessive-compulsive symptoms. Due to the high degree of comorbidity, it is possible that these disorders (obsessional disorder and tic disorder) have a common genetic relationship.

The issue of the comorbidity of OCD and schizophrenia in the research literature has attracted the attention of many researchers, but due to significant differences in the findings of various studies, no consistent results have been reported. Most clinical experts and researchers believe that OCD is more common in an individual with schizophrenia than in the general population. But the exact amount varies greatly between studies. The rate of OCD in schizophrenia has been reported from 7.8% - 41% (Attiullah et al., 2000).

This difference may be due to different methods of screening OCD symptoms or conflicting criteria in the definition of OCD or obsessive-compulsive symptoms (Hudak, 2011). Early research on the association between OCD and depression focused on whether OCD should be considered a mood disorder.

With the progress we have made in understanding the distinctive biological-psychological features of OCD, this question is less likely to be asked. What is more important today is the consequence of depression combined with an obsession with the process and treatment of OCD. Although OCD usually precedes major depression, there is also evidence that some patients with major depression are at risk for developing obsessive thoughts (Schatzberg et al., 1998, Stein and Hollander, 2003).

However, the possible differences between primary and secondary OCD in these groups have not been well defined. In Epidemiological Catchment Area study (ECA), there was evidence that patients with OCD who had other comorbid disorders had certain distinguishing characteristics, such as a higher rate of mild cognitive impairment (Hollander et al., 1996). Fortunately, patients with OCD who also have depression respond well to standard OCD treatments (Zitterl et al., 2000). Although, in some cases, a single treatment may be effective for OCD but not for depression and vice versa (Schaller et al., 1998 ;Stein and Hollander, 2003).

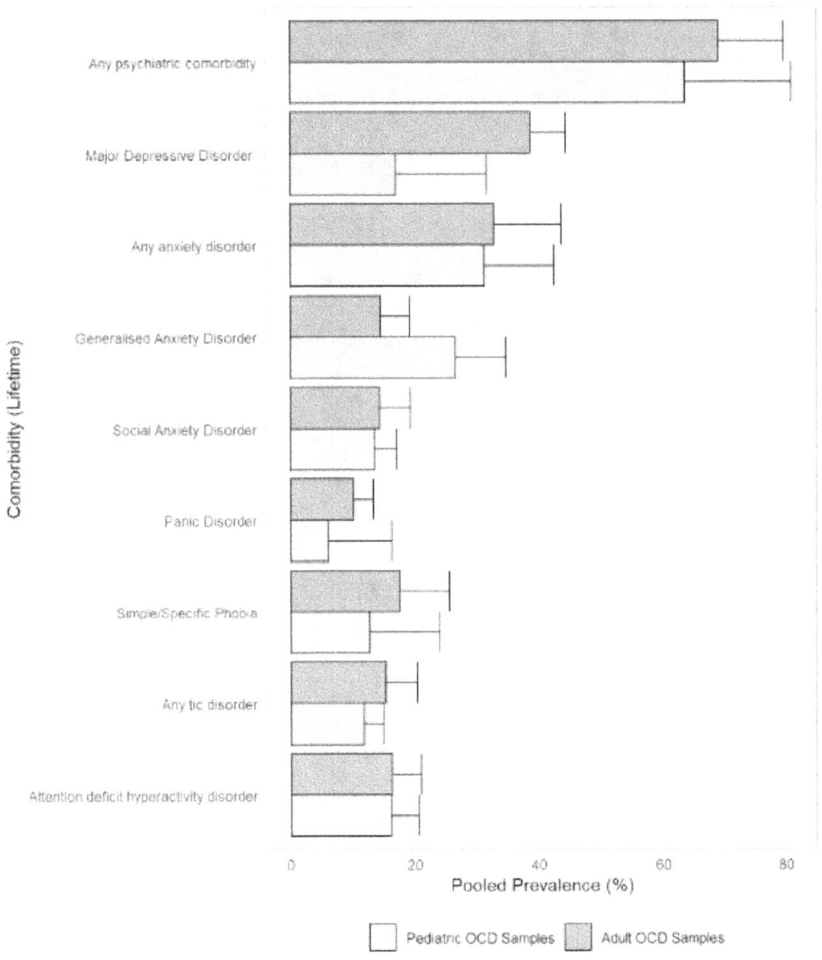

Fig 1. Pooled prevalence rates by comorbidity in adult and paediatric subgroups. (Sharma, E. et al, 2021).

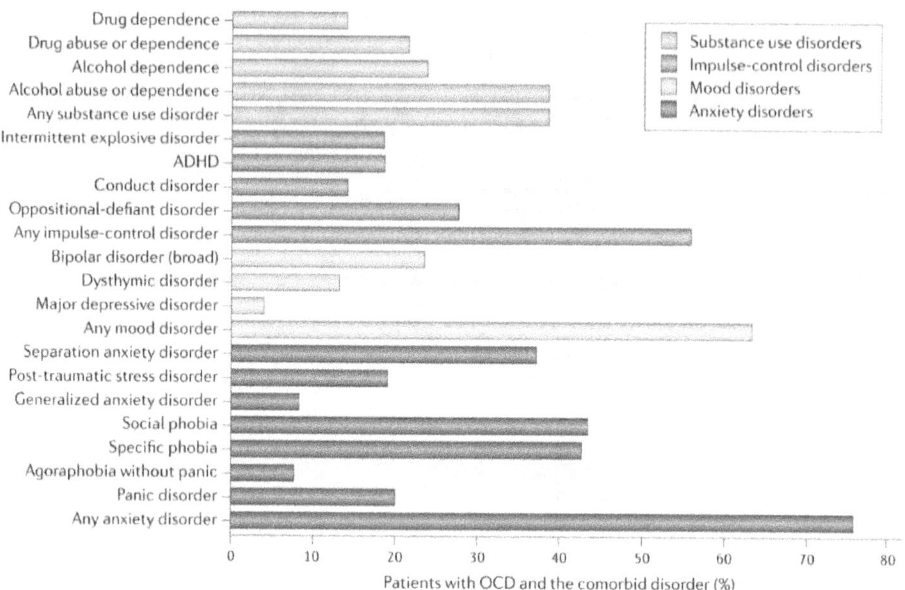

Fig. 2. Comorbidities of OCD. The prevalence of comorbid mental disorders in patients with obsessive–compulsive disorder (OCD) in the National Comorbidity Survey-Replication (NCS-R). ADHD, attention-deficit/hyperactivity disorder. (Stein, D.J. et al, 2020).

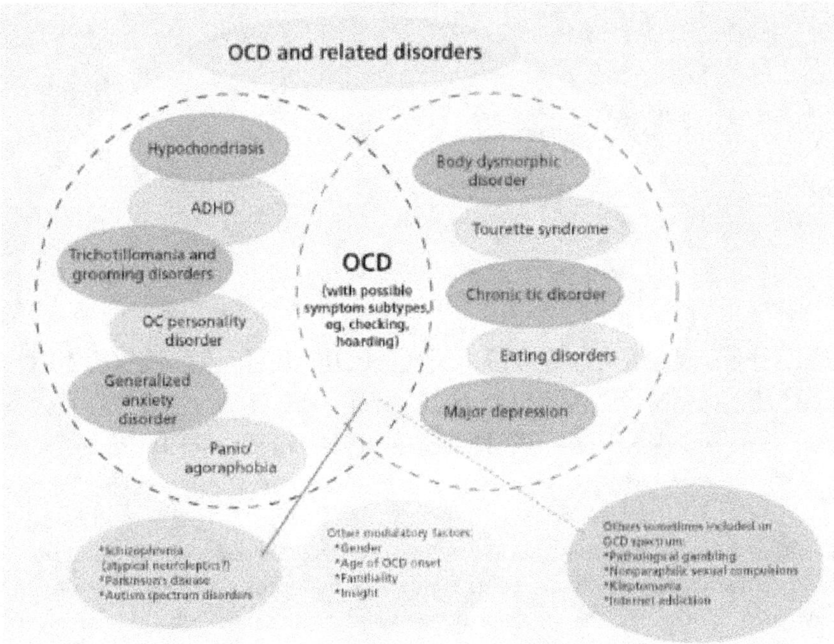

Fig 3. OCD and disorders comorbid with OCD (Murphy, D.L. et al, 2010).

4. BEHAVIORAL AND PSYCHOLOGICAL FACTORS INFLUENCING THE DEVELOPMENT OF THE OBSESSIVE-COMPULSIVE DISORDER

According to the learning theory, which states that obsessive thoughts are conditioned stimuli, a relatively neutral stimulus becomes associated with fear and anxiety through the process of respondent conditioning and pairing it with events that are naturally harmful and anxiety-provoking. In this way, previously neutral thoughts and objects become conditioned stimuli with the power to arouse anxiety and discomfort. Obsessive behavior occurs in a different way. A person finds that a certain action reduces the anxiety associated with an obsessive thought. The release and peace resulting from the removal of anxiety, which acts as a negative driver as a result of the occurrence of obsessive behavior, strengthen this behavior. Gradually, this action becomes a fixed learned behavior pattern due to its usefulness and reduction of a painful secondary driver (anxiety). Learning theory provides useful concepts to explain some aspects of the obsessive-compulsive phenomenon. For example, the anxiety-inducing power of thoughts that are not necessarily frightening and the establishment of obsessive patterns of behavior. Obsessive-compulsive disorder is different from an obsessive-compulsive personality disorder. The majority of patients with the obsessive-compulsive disorder do not have obsessive-compulsive symptoms before the disease, so such traits are neither necessary nor sufficient for the emergence of obsessive-compulsive disorder. Only about 15 to 35 percent of these patients had obsessive traits before the disease. Sigmund Freud initially called what we call OCD today "obsessional neurosis."

He hypothesized that there is a defensive retreat in the appearance of anxiety-provoking oedipal desires. In his opinion, a patient with obsessive-compulsive disorder regresses to the anal stage of psycho-motor development. Freud's theories are discussed below.

Psychodynamic insight may be of great help in understanding treatment compliance issues, interpersonal problems, and personality issues associated with Axis I disorder. Many patients with OCD do not show interest and cooperate with effective treatments such as serotonin reuptake inhibitors (SSRIs) and behavioral therapy. Even if OCD symptoms are influenced by biological factors, a psychodynamic concept is also related to it. Patients may be motivated to maintain their symptoms for secondary benefit. For example, a male patient whose mother stays at home to take care of him may unconsciously continue to have OCD symptoms because he somehow attracts his mother's attention.

Another component of understanding psychodynamic is related to interpersonal relationships. Studies show that Individuals around them coordinate with the OCD patient through active participation with rituals or significant adjustments to their daily schedule. This type of family adaptation is correlated with family stress, rejecting attitude toward the patient, and poor family functioning. Often, family members try to reduce the patient's anxiety or control his anger. This pattern of communication may be internalized and recreated when the patient enters a therapeutic context. By looking at the pattern of interpersonal relationships from a psychodynamic perspective, patients may discover how their illness affects others. Finally, another component of psychodynamic thinking is to recognize the factors that accelerate the onset and exacerbation of symptoms. Interpersonal problems often increase the patient's anxiety and consequently increase his symptoms.

Research suggests that OCD may increase under the influence of certain environmental stressors, especially those related to pregnancy, childbirth, or childcare. Understanding these stressors may help the physician in the overall treatment plan to reduce the stressful events or their meaning for the patient. In classical psychoanalytic theory, obsessive-compulsive disorder is called "obsessive-compulsive neurosis," and it is considered a regression from the oedipal stage of psychosexual development to the anal stage. Obsessive-compulsive disorder patients are afraid of revenge and the loss of an important, beloved object, and withdraw from the Oedipal situation and retreat to a specific emotional stage with a strong dual feeling that is related to the anal stage. The ambivalence of feeling is related to the rupture of the tender bond between the sex drives and aggression specific to the Oedipal stage. The simultaneous existence of love and hate toward a person leaves a person in doubt and powerless to make a decision. An example of how Freud reviewed the symptoms of OCD is described by Ottofenichel as follows:

The patient, who had not been psychoanalyzed, complained in the first interview of a compulsion to constantly look behind, fearing that he might have left something important behind. These thoughts dominated him, whether he did not notice the coin that fell on the ground, whether he stepped on an insect, or whether an insect fell on its back and needed his help. At the same time, this patient was afraid to touch anything, and whenever he touched something, he had to convince himself that he did not destroy it. He had no time to have fun because his compulsions interfered with his professional activity; at the same time, there was passion and excitement in his life.

House cleaning

He liked to go to his neighbors' houses and clean their houses, just for fun. Another symptom he described was a preoccupation with clothing, his preoccupation with whether his clothes fit him. His self-accepted sexuality played no role in his life. He had sex two or three times a year without any personal interest. Another symptom he later described was that when he was a child, he felt that his mother was a disgusting person and hated to touch her. There was no real reason for this hatred because his mother was lovely and friendly (Sadock et al ,2007).

In this clinical form, the need to be clean and not touch is related to anal sex, and hatred of the mother is a reaction to fears of committing adultery. One of the prominent characteristics of patients with obsessive-compulsive disorder is their mental preoccupation with aggression or cleaning, which is either evident in the content of their symptoms or in the connections behind them. This characteristic and other observations have caused the psychological cause of the obsessive-compulsive disorder to be assumed in the disturbance of natural growth and development in the sadistic-anal stage.

Dual feeling

The duality of feeling is a direct result of the change in the characteristics of impulses. Having a double feeling in the stage of sadistic- anal development is considered as one of the important characteristics of a normal child; that is, the child has both a feeling of love and a strong feeling of hatred towards an object, and these two feelings sometimes seem to exist at the same time. Obsessive-compulsive disorder patients sometimes consciously feel both loves and hate towards an object. This conflict of opposite emotions can perhaps be seen in the behavioral pattern of acting-canceling and paralyzing doubts in choosing, which is seen in many sufferers of this disorder.

Magical thinking

In the phenomenon of magical thinking, retroversion causes more primitive thinking patterns, so that impulses, that is, the actions of the ego as well as the actions of the id, are affected by the retroversion. One of the continuous characteristics of magical thinking is the phenomenon of omnipotence. A person feels that just by thinking about an incident in the external world, he can cause it to happen without physical actions, this feeling causes the obsessive-compulsive patient to be afraid of his aggressive thoughts (Sadock et al ,2007).

In the theory of psychoanalysis, obsessions and compulsions are the same and originate from sexual or aggressive instinctive forces that cannot be restrained due to strict toilet training. Therefore, the patient is fixed in the anal stage.The observed symptoms are the result of the conflict between the id and the defense mechanisms, sometimes the aggressive instincts of the id prevail and sometimes, the defense mechanisms prevail. For example, when obsessive thoughts about killing invade, institutional forces prevail. But most of the time, the observed signs indicate a relatively successful performance of one of the defense mechanisms. For example, a person who is fixed in the anal stage may resist the urge to be dirty and be obsessively neat and orderly due to the reaction formation mechanism. Alfred Adler (1931) believed that obsessive-compulsive disorder is caused by a feeling of inadequacy.

He believed that when children are prevented from achieving a sense of self-sufficiency due to the presence of parents with authoritative or supportive style of upbringing, they develop an inferiority complex and unconsciously turn to obsessive rituals to create a territory for themselves and have control over it and be able to feel adequate and useful there. Adler states that the act of obsession allows a person to finally master something. Behavioral explanations about compulsions are such that they are considered learned behaviors that are reinforced through the reduction of fear. For example, obsessive hand washing is an active avoidance response that reduces mental preoccupation and fear of contamination with microbes and dirty things. In the same way, obsessive check-ups can reduce the patient's anxiety caused by the expected disasters that will occur if there is no check-up. In fact, the level of anxiety that is reflected in self-assessment tests as well as the psycho-physiological responses of the patient as a result of obsessive behavior, is reduced. According to this view, the very high frequency of compulsions is due to the fact that differentiating the stimuli that produce anxiety is quite difficult. For example, it is very difficult to know when microbes are still present and when they are removed by washing rituals.

Another view about obsessive checking is that this behavior is due to some kind of memory weakness. Inability to accurately recall certain actions (such as turning off the gas) or to distinguish between real and imagined behavior (perhaps I just think that I turned off the gas), can cause a person to repeatedly check. Although such Individual believe that they have poor memory, the results of laboratory research on certain action-related memory negate this issue.

In a study, panic disorder was compared between two groups of patients with OCD and normal Individual using a general knowledge test. There was no difference between these groups in terms of the number of correct answers. However; patients with OCD had less confidence in their answers than normal Individuals. So if memory has an association with OCD, it seems the main problem is related to trust one's memory, not a memory defect.

What justification do we have for obsessive thoughts? The obsessions of patients with OCD usually make them anxious and are somewhat similar to the disturbing thoughts of normal Individual about stress-causing stimuli, such as stimuli that are watching a horror movie.

Many Individuals sometimes get involved in unwanted thoughts, which in terms of content are like obsessive thoughts. When Individual are exposed to psychological pressure, these undesirable thoughts increase.

Normal Individual are able to tolerate or repel these thoughts. But for obsessive Individual, these thoughts can have certain clarity and cause severe anxiety and worry. Maybe because of childhood experiences that taught them some thoughts are dangerous or unacceptable. Also, obsessive Individual are unable to ignore stimuli which can play a significant role in causing their problems.Individuals with obsessive-compulsive disorder may actively suppress such intrusive thoughts, which can have negative consequences. Wegner and colleagues (1987-1991) investigated what happens when Individual are asked to inhibit a particular thought. In this study, which was conducted on two groups of students, one group was asked to think about a white bear and the other group was told not to think about it. The first group first thought about the white bear and then they were told to stop thinking. The other group did the opposite. Their level of thinking was measured based on the participants expressing these thoughts and also asking them to ring a bell when they thought about the white bear. This research had two significant findings. First, trying not to think about the white bear was not entirely successful. Second, the students who had stopped thinking about the white bear at first thought about it more after the abstinence condition ended. Therefore, trying to avoid thinking about something may have the opposite effect, i.e. causing preoccupation with it. In addition, the suppression of unpleasant thoughts is typically associated with intense emotional states, thereby strengthening the association of the suppressed thought with mentioned emotion.After a lot of effort to suppress, the same strong emotion can call the mentioned thought again and therefore, raise the negative mood. As a result, anxiety will also increase. Cognitive explanations for OCD are similar to those given by Adler. It has been hypothesized that OCD (or at least compulsion) results from an irrational need to feel adequate, or even complete, which causes the individual to feel worthless

The world is seen as a threatening place, and if one feels that there are limits to one's ability to cope with imagined dangers, the only way to achieve a sense of containment and adequacy is through obsessive magical rituals. Another cognitive theory emphasizes underlying assumptions (similar to those made by Ellis), for example, the belief that one should be able to stop harming others or to be in control of one's thoughts (Davison et al. 2004).

It is very common for a person to have disturbing thoughts.What happens if the meat is rotten? What if things are contaminated? What happens if the TV is on when I go out? What happens if I leave the gas on? Most of us are familiar with such thoughts and most of us can deal with them without too much trouble. We get a little anxious, but anxiety does not dominate our behavior. But in such a situation, something very different happens to Individual with OCD. Basically, when a person is prone to OCD symptoms, they become very anxious when faced with such thoughts. There is a basic need to reduce anxiety as a result of obsessive thoughts in (obsessive) Individual, and eliminating this need is achieved through compulsions.

We know that when doing something makes you feel better, you keep doing it. So every time you do the compulsion, because you feel better (as a result of reduced obsessive-compulsive anxiety), your behavior is reinforced and you're likely to do it more. The unfortunate fact is that although compulsions make you feel better in the short term, they do not make you feel better in the long term.

The more you do compulsions, the more you need to do them. The onset of OCD may be when controlling something or washing your hands carefully happens only once, but when these actions continue, this simple assurance (to do the actions accurately) disrupts the routine process and you for feeling better need to do more and more until you are almost completely out of control of what you are doing. You may even perform compulsions in your mind instead of in the outside world. You will never get the chance to find out what you are really afraid of happening by doing obsessive things. Individual often recognize that their worries are somewhat unrealistic, but the only way to really find out is to bravely face them without obsessing.

Obsessions cause anxiety. Compulsions such as washing and checking persist because they seem to reduce or prevent anxiety.Although compulsions may slightly reduce anxiety, in the long term it maintains the obsession and the urge to repeat compulsions by reinforcing the reduction of anxiety (Brosan et al., 2010).

Like those who have panic disorder, Individual who have certain cognitive and behavioral vulnerabilities in addition to biological vulnerability are affected by acute and full-scale types of obsession. Cognitive and behavioral theorists believe that the reason why obsessive Individual can hardly get rid of obsessive thoughts is due to tendencies related to strong and rigid moral thoughts. Since they consider their own negative and stupid thoughts more unacceptable than others, they feel more anxious and guilty. Then this same anxiety makes it more difficult to expel thoughts.Obsessives may believe that they should be able to control their thoughts and may also fail to recognize that everyone may experience negative thoughts from time to time.

This group of Individual believe that having such thoughts is a sign of losing their mind, or that having such thoughts is equal to their actualization (when I think of hurting my child, I am as guilty as if I actually hurt him). The effect of such a way of thinking is surely more anxiety, which makes it more difficult to expel those thoughts. Compulsions may be created in such a way that the person who is suffering from obsessive thoughts sees that certain actions will reduce the obsessive thought and related anxiety, as a result, the reduction of anxiety will strengthen the behavior and compulsions will appear, then every time the thought Obsession comes, they feel that must show that behavior to reduce their anxiety.

In this case, some of the most telling evidences supporting the cognitive and behavioral approaches to obsession have been obtained from the effective treatments resulting from these approaches.In contrast, treatments based on psychoanalytic theories have not been effective. Psychoanalytic theories consider obsessions to be unacceptable impulses (hostility, destructiveness, and inappropriate sexual impulses) that were repressed and now reveal in a transformed form. The person does not know them from himself and these symptoms may be an obsessive behavior to restore and compensate them. A mother who is obsessed with killing her child feels that she has to check the child many times at night to see if he is healthy or not. Obsession rituals also keep threatening impulses away from a person's consciousness; a person who is constantly busy (by compulsions) will not have time for inappropriate thoughts or actions. The theory of psychoanalysis is that the treatment of obsessive-compulsive disorder is possible by revealing unconscious conflicts and gaining insight into them. Although the research in this field is small, it shows that insight-oriented treatments often do not improve obsessions (Hilgard et al, 2014). The important role of purely behavioral approaches in understanding and treating OCD should not be ignored. The behavioral theory of OCD was presented based on the learning theory; especially based on Mowrer's two-factor model of fear and avoidance (1939,1960). According to this model, naturally intrusive thoughts, perceptions, or impulses become associated with anxiety through classical conditioning, such that whenever an intrusive thought comes to mind, anxiety increases. Then, through operant conditioning, the person learns to expel or avoid the stimulus that evokes obsessive thoughts in order to reduce the anxiety caused by obsession.

In this way, the obsessive behavior is done to avoid the anxiety caused by the obsession, and it is negatively reinforced by reducing the anxiety. But obsessive anxiety never disappears. Solomon and Wynne (1954) in a series of experiments on dogs showed that escape and avoidance responses to classically conditioned stimuli are very resistant to disappearance and persist for a long time after cessation. The association of conditioned stimuli with aversive consequences continues. Also, escape and avoidance responses, similar to compulsions seen in OCD patients, became stereotyped behaviors. There are several strengths in the behavioral model. First, this model has empirical support.As shown in a series of classic experiments, exposure to obsessive stimuli increases anxiety and performing compulsions decreases this anxiety. Second, the behavioral approach is based on the assumption that the learning processes involved in the persistence of OCD are normal and there is nothing inherently pathological about the occurrence of unwanted intrusive thoughts. The finding that 90% of Individual experience unwanted intrusive thoughts with similar content (obsessions) supports this view. Third, effective exposure and response prevention (ERP) therapy for OCD is derived directly from this model and the belief that OCD patients have developed avoidance habits that prevent the natural extinction of obsessive-compulsive anxiety. exposure and response prevention(ERP) include: a) confronting the stimuli that cause distress and obsessive anxiety and b) helping to resist the urges in order to escape and avoid that create compulsions. This treatment is highly effective, with an estimated 75% of individuals significantly improving with this treatment and maintaining this improvement at follow-up (eg, Franklin and Foa, 2002: Shafran, 2005).

However, the limitations of exposure and response prevention (ERP) therapy should also be taken into account, which include: a large number of patients did not accept this treatment due to the possibility of confronting the fears caused by obsessions, or stopping before the scheduled time from continuing the treatment (Stanley and Turner, 1995). The efficacy and effectiveness of this treatment are likely to be significantly lower for patients who exhibit obsessive thoughts without manifesting compulsions (Rachman, 1997).

In addition to the aforementioned limitations of behavioral therapy, the behavioral theory has been criticized for its inability to distinguish between the theoretical conceptualizations of the range of anxiety disorders (Salkovskis, 1998). Also, this theory does not explain some clinical phenomena specific to OCD, such as the fact that the presence of a therapist has been observed to reduce obsessive-compulsive anxiety and obsessive-compulsive checking. These reasons, in addition to the fact that obsessions are cognitive phenomena, have led to attention to cognitive components as an important element in the occurrence and content of intrusive thoughts (Salkovskis,1999; Shafran, 2005)

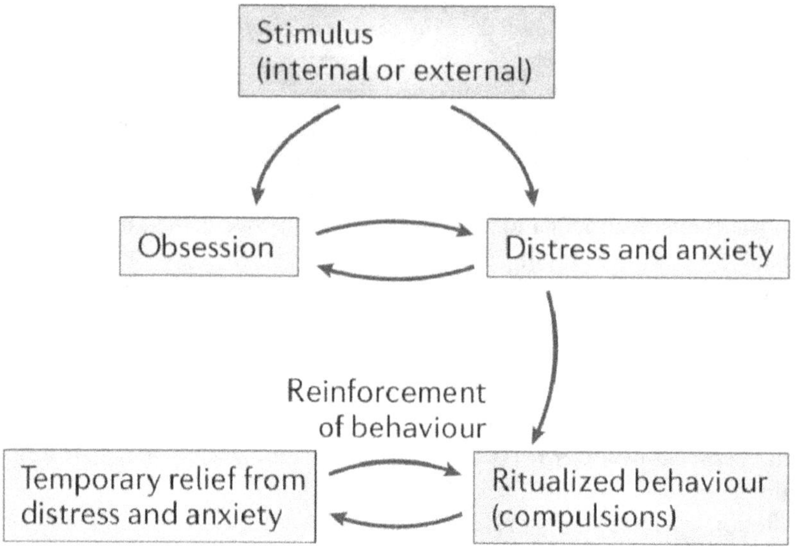

Fig.1. **The theoretical basis of obsessive–compulsive behaviour.** An individual with obsessive–compulsive disorder experiences exaggerated concerns about danger, hygiene or harm that result in persistent conscious attention to the perceived threat or threats; in other words, they result in obsessions. In response to the distress and/or anxiety associated with these obsessions, the person acts (that is, performs a behaviour) to neutralize the distress and/or anxiety, which provides temporary relief from the anxiety associated with the obsession. However, this relief leads to reinforcement of the behaviours, leading to repetitive, compulsive behaviour when obsessions recur. (Pauls , D.L. et al ,2014).

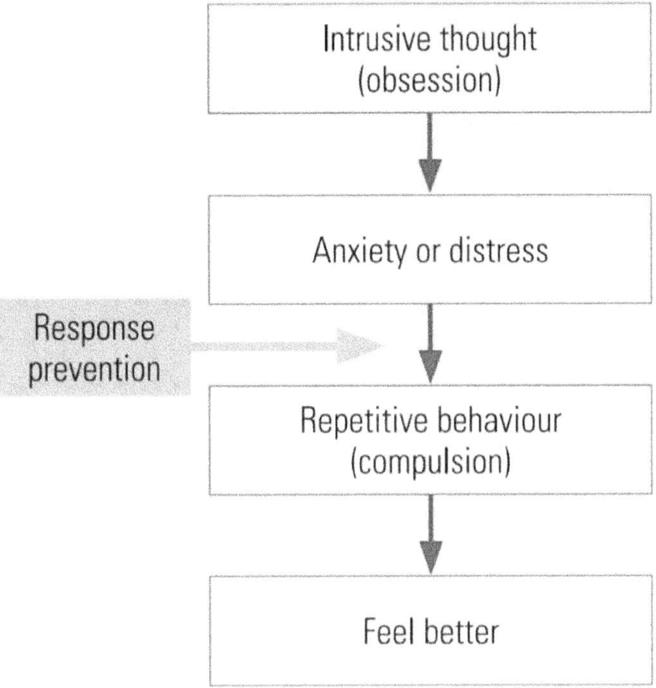

Fig 2. Behavioural treatment of obsessive–compulsive disorder: response prevention aims to break the link between the emotional changes and the compulsions. (Williams,T.I & Shafran, R. 2015).

5. THE ROLE OF GENETICS
IN OBSESSIVE-COMPULSIVE DISORDER

The relative contribution of genes and environment in the development of the obsessive-compulsive disorder is not clearly defined. Studies have shown that more than 10% of parents of Individual with OCD meet the diagnostic criteria for OCD.

Twin studies showed a genetic component in obsessive-compulsive disorder, but this genetic component is a general predisposition to anxiety, not just OCD. The genetic component of this disorder is insignificant compared to other anxiety disorders (Eley et al., 2003: Williams and Waite, 2009). In recent years, there has been an increasing emphasis on research on the effects of mental health problems of parents and its effect on children. In "top-down" studies, children of parents with OCD have been investigated.Black et al. (2003) showed in their two-year follow-up study that children of parents with OCD are likely to show an emotional disorder that is not necessarily OCD.

In other "bottom-up" studies that examined parents of children with OCD, as well as the study by Derisley et al. (2005), was observed that children with OCD were more likely to have parents with a an anxiety disorder. In addition, in these studies, little evidence was found about the transmission (inheritance) of OCD.

However, Hanna et al., (2005) found higher rates of OCD in close relatives of children with OCD compared to close relatives of children without a diagnosis of OCD. While distant relatives did not show higher rates of OCD, these studies showed a minor role of heredity (in OCD) (Williams and Waite, 2009).

Genetic data on OCD are consistent with the hypothesis that the inheritance of this disorder has a significant genetic component. However, these data have not yet determined the influence of cultural and behavioral factors in the transmission of the disorder. Twin comparative studies for OCD have consistently shown higher correspondence rates in monozygotic twins compared to dizygotic twins. Family studies of patients with obsessive-compulsive disorder showed that 35% of immediate relatives of patients with obsessive-compulsive disorder have this disorder. Electrophysiological, sleep electroencephalogram, and neuroendocrine studies indicated the existence of commonalities between obsessive-compulsive disorder and depressive disorders. In patients with obsessive-compulsive disorder, higher abnormalities were observed in the electroencephalogram (EEG). In EEG studies of sleep, abnormalities similar to those seen in depressive disorders, such as decreased rapid eye movement (REM) latency, were observed.

Neuroendocrine studies also showed similarities with depressive disorders. As previously mentioned, studies indicate a possible relationship between a group of OCD cases and some types of motor tic syndromes (such as Tourette's disorder and chronic motor tics).

The rate of chronic motor tics and OCD in the relatives of patients with Tourette's disorder was higher than the relatives of the control group, whether they had OCD or not. Most of the family studies of the first samples with OCD showed a higher rate of Tourette's disorder and chronic motor tics only among the relatives of individuals with OCD who also had some kind of tic disorder. These data indicate a familial and possibly genetic relationship between Tourette's disorder and chronic motor tics, and some types of OCD (Sadock et al ,2007).

One to two percent of the population has obsessive-compulsive disorder (OCD), which is characterized by obsessive thoughts and intrusive impulses, and repetitive compulsions. OCD etiology theory has moved from psychodynamic conflict during the 20th century to considering OCD as a neuropsychiatric disease with an underlying neurobiological abnormality. This trend has occured especially in the last two decades. Therapeutic advances, brain imaging and pharmacological research results have led to the revision of OCD theories of etiology and the creation of new research paradigms.While the response of OCD symptoms to drug treatments and neuroimaging findings that specific brain regions may be involved in OCD suggest a biological etiology (in OCD), family studies suggest a genetic etiology. A genetic etiology has been proposed for OCD based on several factors, including:

1 Twin studies have found higher correspondence rates among monozygotic (MZ) twins than dizygotic (DZ) twins.
2. Higher incidence of OCD among biological (physical) offsprings of individual with this disorder even when they were separated from their parents and raised in adoptive families and their step-parents did not have OCD.
3. Family studies showed a significant concentration of the disorder among family members compared to the prevalence rate in the population (other members of the society).
4. Segregation analysis (genes) confirms the existence of a major gene (for OCD), and
5. Linkage and association studies (genes) reveal effective genes (in OCD).

Twin studies

A review of OCD studies on twin pairs shows a correspondence rate of about 50-60% for this disorder in twins.

Carey and Gottesman (1981) using Maudsley twins statistics; the rate of correspondence of obsessive-compulsive characteristics among 15 pairs of monozygotic twins (MZ) and in 15 pairs of dizygotic twins (DZ) was 87% and 47% respectively. In a study using Leyton Obsessional Inventory, which was conducted on 419 twin pairs, 44% of obsessive-compulsive traits and 47% of obsessive-compulsive symptoms were reported to be heritable. Inouye (1965) reported an 80% correspondence rate for "obsessional neurosis" among 10 pairs of Japanese monozygotic twins, while the correspondence rate for 4 pairs of dizygotic twins was 50%.In another study, McGuffin and Mawson (1980) reported that pairs of identical twins who were separated and were unaware of each other's problems before the onset of OCD symptoms, nevertheless developed OCD symptoms at the same age. In this pair of twins, started and had a similar process of OCD. Two other twin studies showed that although genetic factors are important in anxiety disorders in general, the contribution of genetics to specific anxiety disorders is ambiguous and not entirely clear. In this regard, it should be noted that monozygotic (MZ) twins, compared to dizygotic (DZ) twins, have a similar pharmacological response to the drugs clomipramine and sertraline. In most of the recent reviews of twin studies conducted by van Grootheest et al. (2005), it was observed that only studies that used a dimensional approach and examined structural equation modelling data have convincingly shown that obsessive-compulsive symptoms in children are hereditary, and in this regard, the number of genetic factors was reported as 45% to 65%. Similar studies on adults have shown that the influence of genetics on obsessive-compulsive symptoms ranges from 27% to 47%. For example, in a study conducted by Jonnal et al., (2000) using self-report Padua Inventory of OC symptoms on 527 pairs of twins, the heritability of obsessive thoughts was 33% and compulsions reported by 26 percent.Therefore, although data from twin studies confirm the genetic basis of OCD, it should be noted that in all reported data on twins, the correspondence rate (OCD) for monozygotic (MZ) twins and the heritability estimates are always less than 1 (less than 100%). This situation shows that while genetic factors are important in OCD, this disorder is also affected by environmental factors. In this regard, the analysis of obsessive-compulsive features by Cox et al., (1975) showed a strong association between genetic and environmental factors (Eapen ,2007).

Family studies of OCD

A review of family studies of OCD indicated a significantly higher age-adjusted risk of OCD in parents and siblings of individuals with OCD, which was approximately 35% in first degree relatives (FDRS) (Eapen and Robertson, 2002).

In the 1930s, Lewis et al. (1935) reported a 32.7% prevalence of obsessive-compulsive features in a sample of 306 first-degree relatives (persons with the obsessive-compulsive disorder).

Since then, several family studies have reported significantly higher rates of OCD in parents and siblings of individuals with OCD. This rate is 5 to 10 times higher among parents (obsessed persons) compared to prevalence estimates in the general population. The research results of Rasmussen and Tsuang (1986) showed that 4.5% of parents of patients with OCD had full OCD criteria based on DSM III, while 11.4% had probable obsessive-compulsive disorder or obsessive-compulsive features. In a study of 145 first degree relatives of 46 children and adolescents with OCD, Lenane et al. (1990) reported that 35% of first degree relatives were at an age-adjusted risk of OCD.

Riddle et al. (1990) found in a clinical sample of children with OCD that 71% had a parent with an obsessive-compulsive disorder or obsessive-compulsive symptoms.

Other studies have investigated the role of genetic factors in anxiety disorders generally and reported that an anxiety disorder usually transmits in families with OCD, but the appearance of this anxiety disorder in these families is variable.

In this regard, Black et al. (1992) examined first degree relatives of 32 adults with OCD and 33 psychiatrically normal individuals as a control group. The results showed that the risk of suffering from anxiety disorders among the relatives of individuals with OCD is high compared to the relatives of the control group, but there was no risk of suffering from OCD. The risk of suffering from obsessive-compulsive disorder was high among the parents of individuals with OCD, but among the parents of the control group, this increased risk did not exist (16% vs. 3%).In a study conducted by Bellodi et al. (1992) on 21 patients with OCD whose age of onset was less than 14 years, was shown that the risk of developing the disease among first-degree relatives of this Individual is 8.8%, while this risk was 3.45% among the relatives of 71 patients whose disease onset age was after 14 years. Similarly, Pauls et al. (1995) reported a 10.3% risk of developing the disease among first-degree relatives of Individual with OCD for obsessive-compulsive disorder and 7.9% for OCD that does not meet all diagnostic criteria; this risk was 1.9% and 2% for the control group, respectively. In addition, Nestadt et al. (2000) reported similar values of 11.7% among first-degree relatives of patients with OCD compared to 2.7% for control subjects.

A study conducted by Fyer et al. (2005) showed a significantly higher risk for OCD but not for other anxiety disorders, and in a subsequent study in the same group (Lipsitz, Mannuzza and Chapman et al.,2005) Evidence of familial OCD was found only when the diagnostic threshold included cases of probable OCD or OCD symptoms (and not full-blown OCD). As mentioned earlier, OCD is also related to Tourette syndrome (TS), and there is a view that OCD constitutes another phenotypic of Tourette syndrome (TS). Pauls et al. (1995), in a family study, showed that the frequency of OCD without tics was significantly higher in first-degree relatives of individuals with both Tourette syndrome and obsessive-compulsive disorder and individuals who only had Tourette syndrome without the obsessive-compulsive disorder, and this rate increases in the estimates of the general population and the control group of adopted relatives.In studies that have examined the relationship between the age of onset of OCD in Individuals with this disorder and their relatives with OCD, it was found that more relatives of Individual with OCD whose OCD onset is in childhood are diagnosed with this disorder (Compared to individuals with a higher age of onset of OCD) and individuals with a lower age of onset (childhood) may represent an influential subgroup (of OCD disorder) with more genetic factors and vulnerability to chronic tic disorders (do Rosario-Campos, Leckman andCuri et al., 2005).

The results of the study by Bellodi et al. (1992) as well as the Hopkins family study of OCD showed that the younger age of onset of OCD in affected Individual and more relatives with this disease in their family is related. The study of Hemmings et al. (2004) that reported a clinical association between a young age of onset of the disease and a higher frequency of tics and related disorders, supports from this theory. They also reported a genetic association between early-onset OCD and the dopamine receptor type 4 (DRD4) gene, suggesting a role for the dopaminergic system in early-onset OCD (childhood OCD) as opposed to the serotonergic system involved in the development of adult OCD.Furthermore, examining the co-morbidity studies of OCD with tic disorders may be a confirmation to consider important clinical subgroups (of OCD) with different neurobiological and phenomenological mechanisms (Eapen, Yakely, Robertson 2005). Eapen et al. (1997) in a family study of individuals with OCD and individuals with OCD plus Tourette's syndrome found that all individuals with OCD who had symptom profiles similar to individuals with Tourette's syndrome had at least a first-degree relative with OCD, while none of the affected individuals in the other group had a positive family history. These researchers acknowledged that the latter group could be considered non-familial or individual cases. Lochner et al. (2004) in a cluster analysis study detected three separate groups at the level of 1/1 distance and at the same time found that none of these groups were associated with another specific genetic type. The lack of genetic confirmation of these groups may indicate clinical and genetic heterogeneity in obsessive-compulsive disorder (OCD) and the role of other genes that have not been investigated so far. In fact, the familial basis of different clinical symptom dimensions has been suggested for OCD. Bhattacharyya et al. (2005) in a family study proposed the family basis of the checker (controlling) subtype.Denys et al. (2004) in a factor analysis study determined five dimensions of consonant symptoms including pollution and cleaning; violent, religious and sexual obsessions; checking and physical obsessions; Compulsions with symmetry, counting and order; and the assessment of being at risk with significant differences in the distribution of gender, age of onset and family prevalence of obsessive-compulsive disorder. Also, Leckman et al. (2003) in another study in a sample of Individual with Tourette's syndrome with OCD (both with Tourette's syndrome and OCD) revealed evidence of the effects of the dominant major gene in obsessions with symmetry, order and obsessions and checking. These findings suggest that these types of obsessions may form genetically significant subgroups of OCD.In this regard, three subgroups of obsessive-compulsive disorder were determined: 1- familial OCD, 2- familial OCD related to Tourette syndrome and tic disorders, and 3- non-familial OCD (Eapen, Yakely, Robertson, 2005). These results may support genetic heterogeneity in both OCD and Tourette syndrome (Eapen, 2007).

Gene segregation analysis

When twin studies suggested the possibility of genetic transmission (inheritance) and family studies suggested a higher probability of relatives being affected (disease), segregation analysis (genes) can determine which traits and characteristics in families are consistent with genetic models.

Using computer programs (for example, SEGRAN and POINTER), different genetic models (such as dominant, recessive, mixed, polygenic, etc.) were investigated and the hypotheses were tested using the likelihood ratio test (LRT), by estimating the difference in values (logarithm -2 (L)+K) have been tested for a specific hypothetical model in which (L) is a probability coefficient and (K) is a constant value. The most suitable model was assigned a value of 0.0 and all other models with positive deviation from this model (the best model) were presented.

Nicolini et al. (1991) reported a dominant pattern of inheritance with 80% prevalence in 24 families of individuals with OCD, chronic motor tics (CMT), and Tourette syndrome (TS) using segregation analysis. In another discriminant analysis study on families with OCD, Cavallini et al. (1999) conducted discriminant analysis on a sample of 107 families with OCD and reported a dominant model of transmission with a higher prevalence for women. Alsobrook et al. (1999) in a discriminant analysis study using factor-analytic symptom dimensions of family sample based on symptom scores of affected individuals concluded that relatives of families with high scores in symmetry and order symptoms are exposed to are at a higher risk of developing OCD.In addition, Nestadt et al. (2000) in the study of Hopkins, using 153 families (80 families as the experimental group and 73 families as the control group) showed the most appropriate gender-dependent dominant model and more transmission (reported disease) in women. Eapen et al. (2006) conducted a discriminant analysis using information obtained from 66 first-degree relatives of 20 families of Individual with OCD and provided evidence for a major locus mode of OCD transmission. Therefore, although the available evidence obtained from discriminant analysis studies shows that the family transmission of OCD is genetic, but the exact mode of transmission has not yet been determined. While some studies have suggested the possibility of the dominant model, but at the same time, the mixed model that includes several genes with a major effect on a multi-gene background cannot be rejected (Eapen, 2007).

Linkage studies

When familial transmission is through a genetic mechanism, the next step is to perform linkage analysis to determine the location of the putative major gene within chromosomal segments or hotspots.

This step is based on the assumption that loci located close to each other on the same chromosome are transferred (linked). Linkage analysis is based on meiotic events that determine whether linked genes on the same chromosome will remain the same through recombination. If the genes are separated from each other through recombination, it indicates a difference.

The probability of difference for two genes or a hypothetical gene and a marker is a function of the distance between them. This probability is calculated using a genome-wide marker map that represents the distance between a hypothetical gene location and a known marker.Then, the likelihood ratio of linkage/no-linkage or the probability of the link is calculated and the probability coefficient is expressed with the LOD score or the log of the odds ratio. LOD score (3) {probability 1 / 1000 (3 = logarithm of probability)} is considered as a significant score for accepting the link hypothesis and score (-2) as a significant score for not accepting the link hypothesis. Although the score (3) is considered significant for Mendelian loci, it may not be sufficient for more complex disorders. Weissbecker et al. (1989) reported a LOD score (1/3) in the region of the short arm of chromosome number 4 by studying three generations of a family with OCD and tic disorders. Shugart et al,. (2006) in a genome-wide linkage study with a study of 219 families that were identified in collaboration with the OCD genetics study found evidence for sensitive loci on the long arm of chromosome 3, the short arm of chromosome 7, the long arm of chromosome number 1, the long arm of chromosome number 15 and the long arm of chromosome number 6 along with the strongest evidence for the long arm of chromosome number 3 In addition, the analysis of linkage variables on the possible role of the gene or genes located on chromosome number 1 indicates an increased risk of early onset of OCD.

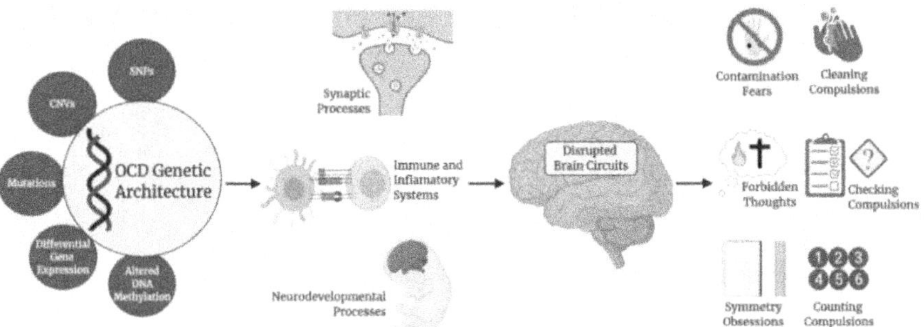

Fig1. From genetic architecture to obsessive-compulsive disorder (OCD) symptomatology. The genetic architecture of OCD presumably underlies alterations in biological pathways, which in turn lead to disrupted brain circuits and OCD symptoms. CNV, copy number variant; SNP, single nucleotide polymorphism.(Saraiva ,L.C. et al, 2020).

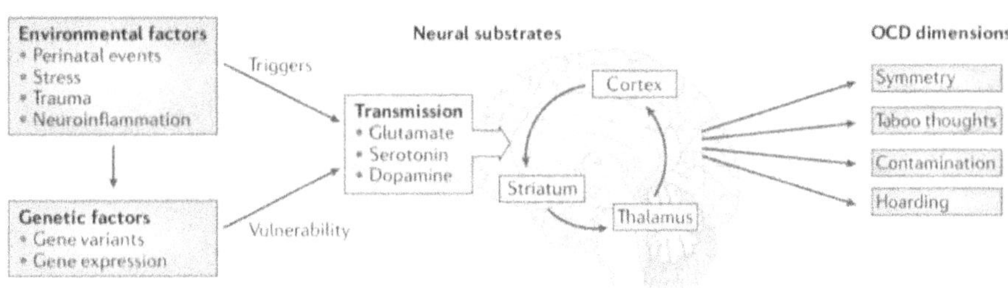

Fig.2. An integrative model of genetics, environment and neurobiology for the expression of OCD. Individuals with obsessive–compulsive disorder (OCD) may be genetically vulnerable to the impact of environmental factors that may trigger modification of the expression of glutamate-, serotonin- and dopamine-system-related genes through epigenetic mechanisms. In turn, neuroanatomical expression of these modifications results in an OCD-specific imbalance between the direct and indirect loops of the cortico–striato–thalamo–cortical (CSTC) circuit. Aberrant activation along the CSTC loop is associated with phenotypic presentation of OCD phenomenology. Although OCD is clinically heterogeneous, it is generally and universally characterized by obsessive concerns about threats or danger and subsequent engagement in rituals to neutralize the threats and/or distress that accompany obsessions. This negative reinforcement cycle, when left untreated, perpetuates OCD psychopathology. (Pauls, D.L. et al ,2014).

6. THE ROLE OF NEUROTRANSMITTERS IN OCD AND ANIMAL MODELS IN THIS REGARD

Neurotransmitter relations undoubtedly play a significant role in determining personality traits and thought processes. Nevertheless, on a more precise analytical level, it can be said that one of the important factors determining the quality of thinking in a person is the processing of information in different neurons. Single neurons communicate by instantaneously converting chemical signals into electrical activity for transmission in axons and ultimately by effectively converting electrical data into precisely regulated chemical secretions by which they influence other neurons or non-neuronal cells, and electrical impulses facilitate immediate responses; therefore, the chemical environment is extremely important to maintain the accuracy and correctness of the brain's perception of the world. The study of chemical interneuron communication is called neurochemistry.

With the acceptance of the neuron theory of Wilhelm His and Santiago Ramon y Kajal in the late nineteenth century, who stated that the brain is composed of individual cells rather than a multinucleated mass of cytoplasm, research began to find intercellular mediators. At the end of the century, the effects of adrenal gland extracts on sympathetic nervous tissue were discovered, and scientists soon introduced neurotransmitter brain chemicals with similar excitatory actions.

Assuming that cells contain both inhibitory and excitatory "receptor substances," Karl Leshley considered all the significant components of chemical transmission: neurotransmitters and specific receptor molecules. In the first half of the 20th century, biogenic amine neurotransmitters were first identified, while the more abundant amino acid neurotransmitters were not recognized as neurotransmitters until recently. In recent years, a high abundance of known peptide neurotransmitters and receptors has been reported, and new classes of neurotransmitters have been defined, including nucleotides, prostaglandins, and gases. In this way, the realm of neurochemistry was mixed with the complexity of the mass of molecules. Its limits were removed from the study of the chemical conversion of nerve impulses and turned into a broad field that overlaps with neurodissection, neurobiology growth, and behavioral genetics (Sadock et al ,2007).

Biological reports of OCD to describe OCD have been associated with general defects in some brain regions or (the etiology of OCD) in differences in neurotransmitters. Studies have focused primarily on serotonin, which is effective in regulating mood, excitement, sleep, and appetite and plays a vital role in controlling physiological and behavioral actions. The finding that certain drugs that act as serotonin reuptake inhibitors (SSRIs) can be effective in reducing OCD symptoms led to the initial hypothesis that serotonin may be abnormal, and studies have reported different levels of serotonin in OCD.

Brain scanning studies have reported biological differences in OCD (compared to normal subjects), for example, different metabolic values in a part of the brain called the frontostriatal system. But only these received differences do not necessarily indicate a defect or abnormality (in the brain system).

Baxter et al. (1992) showed that abnormalities identified by brain scanning could be addressed through behavioral therapy or pharmacotherapy and reported that any neurocognitive changes were reversible. If biological factors cause OCD, then theories (based on biological factors) should explain how treatment can be effective and psychological therapy can be effective (in treating OCD). Theories should also broadly explain the phenomenology of OCD, such as why problems with memory and decision-making occur only in situations relevant to the obsessional issue. To advance the understanding (of OCD), biological accounts of OCD should be able to make specific predictions based on the phenomenology of OCD and provide evidence to evaluate them (Williams and Waite, 2009).

From a therapeutic point of view, OCD is a strange disorder. Because it has been determined that only one type of pharmacotherapy, explicitly affecting the serotonergic system, is beneficial in this case. The direct association of noradrenergic antidepressants with clomipramine or with selective serotonin reuptake inhibitors (SSRI) has anti-obsessive effects. This selective response to pharmacotherapy in Obsessive-compulsive disorder, specifically caused by the modulation of the effect of a neurotransmitter, is unclear in other disorders such as depression, panic disorder, or schizophrenia.

In depression and panic disorders, a set of noradrenergic and serotonergic blockers, such as ECT (Electroconvulsive therapy: for depression) and alprazolam (for panic disorder), are, and in schizophrenia, pharmacotherapy with dopaminergic and serotonergic drugs seems to be effective. In obsessive-compulsive disorder, the reduction of etiological symptoms depends on 5 HTindice, such as metabolic changes of serotonin, 5-HIAA in the cerebrospinal fluid (CSF) and reduction of Serotonin activityin the part of the corpus spheroid But this relationship does not exist in the metabolism of noradrenaline, MHPG, or dopamine HVA.

In addition, the activity of the non-selective serotonin antagonist, metergoline, in patients with OCD who had responded to clomipramine maintained the antiobsessive effect for four days. Such clinical research leads us to hypothesize that OCD as a serotonergic disease. Another condition to confirm this hypothesis is the presence of an abnormality in the serotonin system in the case of obsessive-compulsive disorder. Therefore, the observed behavioral responses are due to the effect of the serotonin agonist, meta-chlorophenylpiperazine (mcpp), which has a composition very -similar to 5 HT2C and 5 HT1D receptors. Also, the results showed that OCD patients experienced a significant amount of anxiety and depression after using meta-chlorophenylpiperazine (mcpp) compared to those who used a placebo.

In addition, the symptoms of obsessive-compulsive disorder in untreated patients and some new individuals or patients whose signs and symptoms were urgently intensified temporarily. These results have not been proven in cases other than serotonergic. The arrangement of the 5-HT receptor subtype has now been identified, and much research has been conducted to determine which subtype may be responsible for OCD. 5-HT$_{1A}$receptor has also been recognized by the lack of effect on OCD symptoms of the 5-HT$_{1A}$ ligand ipsapirone , as well as the failure of buspirone, which is a 5-HT$_{1A}$ agonist, lose their arrangement. These results provide additional therapeutic effects in incremental therapy. In addition, the presence of serotonin agonist (MK-212), which has a very high affinity with 5-HT$_{1A}$ and 5-HT$_{2C}$ receptors, has not had any effect on the behavior of patients with obsessive-compulsive disorder. 5-HT$_2$ receptors are involved in modulating anxiety-related behaviors. In this regard, it has been suggested that the anti-obsessional effect of SSRIS is through their activity in using the neurotransmitter 5-HT (serotonin). This is a finding supported by the experimental results of investigating the impact of clomipramine in increasing the response of cortisol to 5-HT. In addition, it has been shown that the antiobsessive effects of fluvoxamine are reduced by 5-HT$_2$ antagonists and ritanserin. By introducing findings from studies investigating meta-chlorophenylpiperazine (mcpp), MK-212, and ipsapirone, 5-HT$_{2C}$ and 5-HT$_{1D}$ receptors appear more likely to act to relieve symptoms of OCD and exacerbate OCD symptoms with 5-HT$_{1D}$ agonist, Sumatriptan,confirms the role of 5-HT$_{1D}$ in this case. Even though more attention is focused on the postsynaptic serotonin receptor, the complexities of the presynaptic mechanisms should also be considered; because the number of 3-hydroxy imipramine and 3-hydroxy paroxetine receptor sites in patients with obsessive-compulsive disorder who do not receive medication has decreased compared to control groups of other patients with other anxiety disorders. This is despite the fact that treatment with a SSRIS causes a significant increase in the concentration of 3-hydroxy imipramine and may be the transporter of 5-hydroxy tryptamine or 5-HT effect on recovery and reaction to serotonergic drugs. Although serotonin plays a central role in OCD, the pathophysiology of OCD is very complex, and the dysfunctional functioning of more than one transporter is likely involved, and other systems should be investigated. The most substantiated evidence for the involvement of dopaminergic centers in obsessive-compulsive disorder is obtained from the clinical findings of examining the symptoms of obsessive-compulsive disorder in basal ganglia disorders such as Tourette syndrome and Posten cephalitic Parkinson's disease. A close correlation between these disorders and obsessive-compulsive disorder is reported. Meanwhile, the dysfunctional role of dopaminergic centers in obsessive-compulsive disorder has been confirmed with a tic disorder (Montgomery and Zohar,1999). In the rest of this chapter, the role of several essential neurotransmitters in OCD and animal models in this regard will be mentioned.

Serotonin

Serotonin (5-hydroxy tryptamine or 5-HT) is synthesized from the amino acid tryptophan. The function of serotonin (5-HT) is terminated due to its destruction by monoamine oxidase (MAO) and catechol-O-methyltransferase (COMT), and it is converted into inactive metabolites such as 5-hydroxyindoleacetic acid (5-HIAA). Most of the serotonin is metabolized outside the neuron by the enzyme MAO, type MAO_A.

(The MAO_B type has little effect on serotonin and reduces serotonin to a lesser extent). Serotonin has different receptors. Some are presynaptic (such as: $5\text{-}HT_{1B/D}$; $5\text{-}HT_{1A}$) and some are postsynaptic (such as: $5\text{-}HT_{1A}$, $5\text{-}HT_{1B/D}$, $5\text{-}HT_{2A}$, $5\text{-}HT_{2C}$, $5\text{-}HT_3$, $5\text{-}HT_4$, $5\text{-}HT_5$, $5\text{-}HT_6$, $5\text{-}HT_7$).

Presynaptic 5-HT receptors are autoreceptors that regulate 5-HT diffusion and release, while postsynaptic serotonin receptors regulate various neural circuits (McGrath et al., 2000). Therefore, serotonin is related to both excitatory and inhibitory processes. The effect of serotonin on OCD has been investigated in various ways in patients and animal models. Serotonin levels in the cerebrospinal fluid (CSF) of OCD patients have also been specifically studied. Examining the levels of cerebrospinal fluid (CSF) metabolites has raised the question of the relationship between what is found in the cerebrospinal fluid and what is happening in the brain. This question arises not only for serotonin but also for all metabolites measured in CSF. It has been reported that the increase of CSF amines such as serotonin, dopamine, and glutamate is not precisely coordinated with the increased neurotransmitter activity in cortical and subcortical (brain) pathways. Different processes such as diffusion and neurotransmission, glial uptake, diffusion barriers, separation of other metabolic compounds, and degradation may also be involved in changes in cerebrospinal fluid (CSF) neurotransmitter levels. However, several studies have suggested a blood-CSF barrier for amino acids (Rothstein et al., 1992) and reported that neurotransmitter concentrations in cerebrospinal fluid could indicate their function in the central nervous system.

Chou-Green et al. (2003) tested a rat in which the $5\text{-}HT_{2C}$ receptor was deleted. This rat was initially described as a model for obesity. They reported that this experimental rat increased chewing on soil with no food and a distinct cleaning pattern. And the habit of head dipping activity has decreased compared to the wild type. They concluded that the inactivation of the $5\text{-}HT_{2C}$ receptor in rats creates a model for compulsive behavior. These data point to the role of the 5-HT$_{2C}$ receptor in the pathophysiology of this behavior (compulsion). However, the predictive validity of this model for OCD has not been adequately evaluated. Tsaltas et al. (2005) researched a model based on persistence (repetition) in the interval frequency of receiving rewards. Using this behavioral model, these researchers have shown that in this animal model for OCD, 5-HT$_{2C}$ receptors are involved in the primary mechanism of obsessive-compulsive behavior. Acute administration of MCPP (metachlorophenylpiperazine), a non-selective 5-HT receptor agonist, increased obsessive-compulsive behavior. This effect could be prevented by long-term pretreatment with fluoxetine, but diazepam or desipramine had no effect in preventing (compulsion).

Naratriptan, a selective antagonist of 5-HT$_{1B}$ receptors, was not effective in this animal model; the effect of MCPP confirms the role of 5-HT$_{2C}$ receptors. Flaisher-Grinberg et al. (2008) investigated the effects of activation and blockade of 5-HT$_{2A}$ and 5-HT$_{2C}$ in a signal attenuation rat model of OCD.

In this model, obsessive-compulsive behavior is caused by the weakening of the response sign of the effective lever pressure in food production (receiving). Regular use of (RS102221) 5-HT2C antagonist reduced compulsive lever-pressing, whereas regular use of (MDL11, 939) 5-HT2A antagonist or 5-HT$_{2A / 2C}$ agonist DOI had no selective effect on this behavior. Joel and Avisar (2001) created the rat model of OCD based on the hypothesis that the deficient (defective) response feedback mechanism underlies compulsive obsessions behaviors. Rats in the silenced condition of lever pressing for food after weakening external feedback for this behavior exhibited excessive lever pressing without the intention of obtaining a reward (food), which may be similar to the excessive and irrational behavior observed in OCD.

Using this model, Joel et al. (2005) found that damage to the orbital frontal cortex (brain) of rats leads to compulsive lever pressing, which was parallel to the increase in striatal 5-HT (serotonin) transmitter concentration.

This state shows that obsessive-compulsive behavior was associated with changes in the striatal serotonergic system in this model. Also, the predictive validity of this model has been determined considering its response to acute treatment with (Serotonin Reuptake Inhibitors) (SSRI).

In summary, along with some pharmacological challenges and some findings regarding 5-HT (serotonin), many animal models of OCD implicate a specific role for 5-HT in OCD, which needs further investigation (Abudy et al., 2012).

Dopamine

Dopamine is synthesized from the amino acid tyrosine. There are at least five subtypes of dopamine receptors, D_1 through D_5. D_1 and D_5 receptors are members of the D_1-like family of dopamine receptors, while D_2, D_3, and D_4 receptors are members of the D_2-like family. The major metabolite of dopamine breakdown is homovanillic acid (HVA). Joel and Doljansky (2003) demonstrated that administration of the D_1 antagonist SCH23390 reduced the number of obsessive lever presses without affecting the number of lever presses in pursuit of a reward (food). Based on electrophysiological data, these researchers have reported that the compulsion of lever-pressing depends on a gradual decrease in D_1 receptor stimulation. Campbell et al. (1999) have studied the behavioral consequences of transgenic stimulation of the sub-group of dopamine neurons that express the D_1 receptor in the cortex and amygdala on rats of intracellular cholera toxin (CT) origin. This study reports that chronic stimulation of these neurons, including D_1, induces complex obsessive-compulsive behavior similar to OCD symptoms in humans. Although these rats were resistant to behavioral inhibition by the D_1 receptor antagonist and sensitive to the D_2 receptor antagonist sulpiride, Campbell et al. (2000) reported that chronic stimulation of cortical D_1-containing neurons and limbic may cause obsessive and compulsive behaviors. In another animal model for OCD in which rats were chronically treated with the selective $D_{2/3}$ receptor agonist quinpirole (QNP), a series of ritual-like behaviors similar to obsessive-compulsive disorder-checking behavior was observed (Einat and Szechtman, 1995; Szechtman et al., 2001; Abudy et al., 2012). This obsessive-compulsive behavior is functionally dependent on the use of QNP because when the use of QNP is stopped, this obsessive behavior quickly returns to normal behavior (Sullivan et al.,1998). Postmortem analyses in these animals showed increased dopamine levels in the nucleus accumbens and right prefrontal cortex (brain) tissue. Another study (de Haas et al., 2011) qualitatively tested the dimensions of ritualistic compulsive-like behavior behavior in rats induced by quinpirole consumption. It investigated whether the behavioral effects caused by quinpirole sensitization will remain after two weeks of withdrawal (quinpirole) or not and if there is any effect of quinpirole on extracellular dopamine levels in the nucleus accumbens after two weeks of withdrawal. This research obtained the same finding as the previous one; compulsive-like behavior is dependent on the use of quinpirole because this behavior quickly became normal after stopping the use of quinpirole. Unlike OCD rituals, quinpirole-induced behavior involves a smaller set of behaviors. As seen in patients with OCD, animals tested with quinpirole performed these behaviors with a high repetition rate. These findings showed that the behavior caused by quinpirole manifests only a part of the compulsion observed in patients with OCD. Zor et al. (2009) reported that ritual behavior, such as an increase in irrelevant and unnecessary actions in OCD rituals, is related to increased dopamine function in the nucleus accumbens and right prefrontal cortex (brain). In a study on rats, Korff et al. (2008) observed that the attenuation of stereotyped movement can be observed not only with serotonin agonist (MCPP) but also with D_2 agonist. But the well-known models of OCD can be considered models for other disorders, such as tic disorders, grooming, and trichotillomania. In summary, the information obtained from the animal models of OCD that have been examined reports a role for dopamine, especially for D_1 and D_2 receptors, in the primary mechanism of compulsive-like behavior (Abudy et al., 2012).

Glutamate

Glutamate is the most abundant excitatory neurotransmitter in the nervous system of vertebrates (some researchers have estimated that more than 90% of synapses in the human brain contain glutamate). In the postsynaptic cell, glutamate binds to glutamate receptors such as NMDA (N-methyl-D-aspartate) receptor.

McGrath et al. (2000) showed that MK-801, a non-competitive NMDA receptor antagonist that indirectly stimulates cortico-limbic glutamate production, increased tragenically dependent (transgenic) abnormal behavior, Repeated mutation and elevation in the transgenic rat model and the comorbidity of TS (Tourette syndrome) with OCD.

In summary, it is difficult to conclude the role of glutamate in the pathogenesis of OCD, although studies have reported that the glutamate scheme should be further investigated. It is important to note that there is evidence in this area, mainly emerging from family and twin studies, which suggests that genetic risk factors are essential for at least some forms of OCD. Most of the genes that have been investigated are involved in the functioning or malfunctioning of the neurotransmitters mentioned above (Abudy et al., 2012).

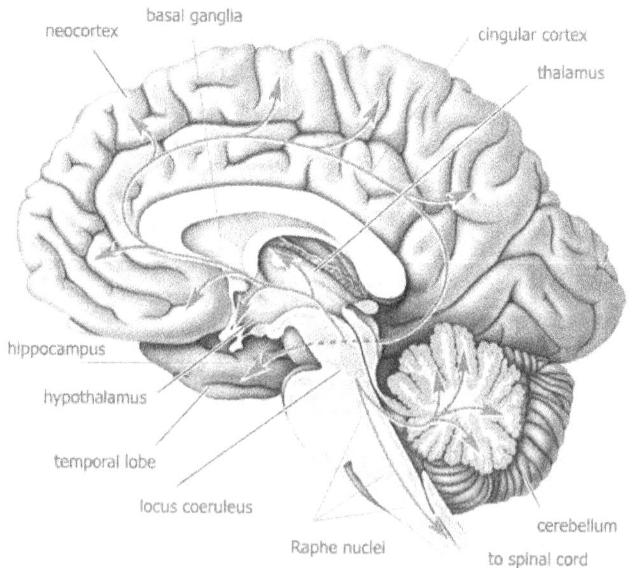

Fig.1. The Serotonin System (Stoler, D.R. 2021).

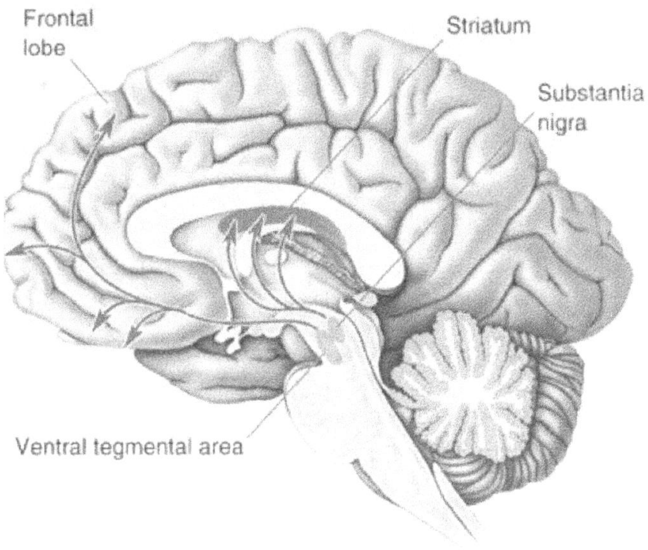

Fig.2. The Dopamine System (Stoler, D.R. 2021).

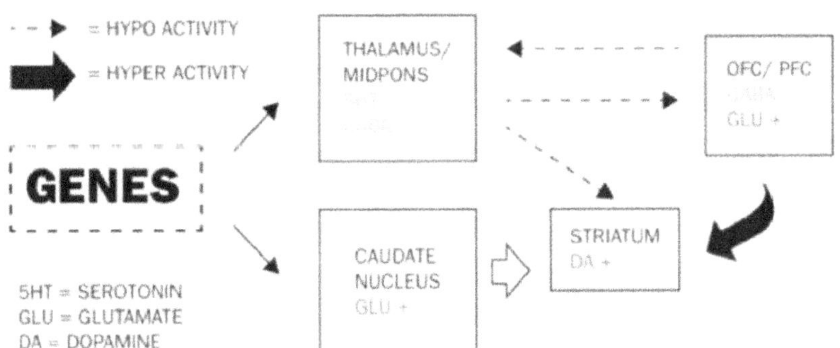

Fig.3. An Integrative Model of Neurotransmitter Dysregulation in OCD This figure highlights the altered functional connectivity in the brain of a patient with OCD, namely the hyperactivity of circuits linking the frontal cortex with the ventral striatum via glutamatergic neurotransmission and dopaminergic neuromodulation, along with the hypoactivity observed in circuits linking the frontal cortex with the thalamus and indirectly with the striatum via serotonergic modulation of glutamatergic and GABAergic neurotransmission. (Graat, Figee and Denys ,2017; Reis ,N.A. 2020).

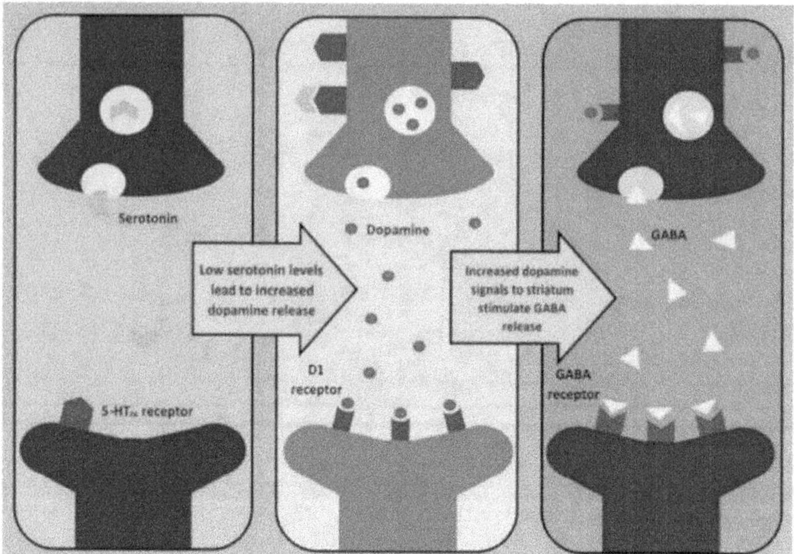

Fig. 4. Downstream interactions of the 3 neurotransmitter systems involved in OCD. In the event of low serotonin levels, possibly occurring as a consequence of low estradiol, the quantities of serotonin are insufficient to inhibit dopamine signaling via 5-HT 2A receptors. This results in increased dopaminergic tone, which has also been identified in some OCD patients. Increased dopaminergic signals from the substantia nigra pars compacta to the striatum, mediated by D1 receptors, increase GABA release from the striatum to the globus pallidus internal and substantia nigra reticulata, thus skewing the cortico-striato-thalamo cortical loop towards the direct pathway.(Karpinski , M. , Mattina ,G.F. , Steiner, M. 2017).

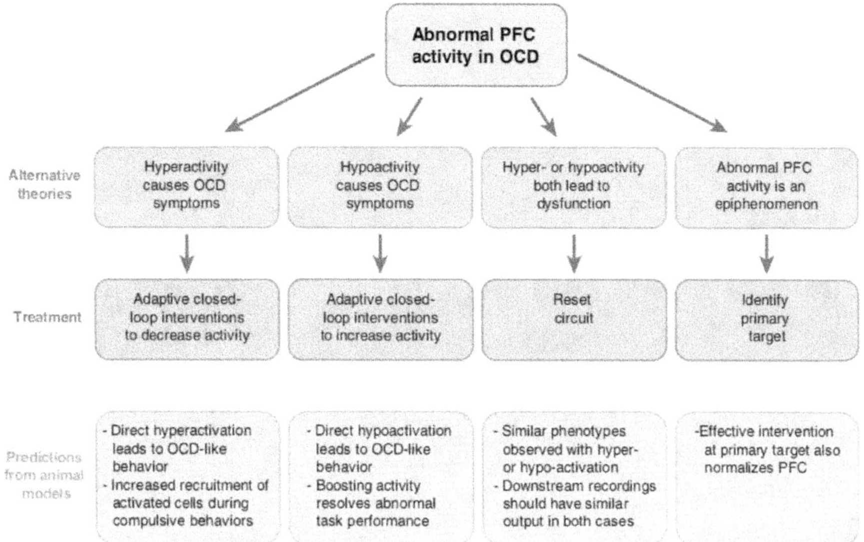

Fig. 5. Alternative theories of how abnormal PFC function could lead to OCD symptoms. Treatments for each of these scenarios and testable predictions from animal models are provided for each theory. (PFC : prefrontal cortex).(Ahmari ,S.E. and Rauch ,S.L. 2022).

Table 1. Behavioral animal models of obsessive-compulsive disorder. KO: Knockout; OFC: Orbitofrontal circuitry; SSRI: Selective serotonin reuptake inhibitors. (Grados, M. et al, 2016).

Behavioral target	Organism	Face validity (behavior)	Construct validity (pathophysiology)	Predictive validity (treatment response)
Collecting behaviors				
Marble burying	Mice	Collecting behaviors	Analog of repetitive digging persistent across exposures and genetically determined	Response SSRIs, memantine, amantadine, aripiprazole, anxiolytics (not desipramine or riluzole)
Nest-building	House mice	Repetitive and collective behaviors	Breed of mice collect large amounts of cotton for nest-building	Nesting and digging response to fluoxetine and clomipramine but not desipramine
Repetitive behaviors				
Spontaneous stereotypy	Deer mice	Naturally occurring repetitive behaviors	Bilateral striatal infusion NMDA or dopamine D1 receptor antagonists selectively reduce stereotypic jumping	Stereotypies respond to fluoxetine but not desipramine; decrease with mCPP and quinpirole
Signal attenuation	Rats	Repetitive behaviors	Post-training signal attenuation stimulus results in less feedback but behavior persists	Responds to SSRIs, D-cycloserine but not to diazepam, desipramine, haloperidol
Reversal learning	5-HT2CR KO mice, non-human primates; rats	Perseverative behaviors	OFC cortex serotonin depletion impairs reversal learning ; 5HT-2C KO mice increase perseveration	5HT-2A antagonist impairs and 5HT-2C antagonist improves reversal learning ; fluoxetine improves perseverative responses
Repetitive biting Behaviors	D1CT7 transgenic mice	Repetitive behaviors	Stereotypies and seizures with higher doses using cortical-limbic dopamine D1 receptor ; increased repetitive climbing and leaping behaviors with glutamate excess (MK801) at cortical-limbic sites ; yohimbine exacerbates abnormal leaping in D1CT mice but not abnormal behavioral perseverance	Not tested

7. BRAIN IMAGING STUDIES OF OCD

Brain and neuroimaging studies have made many changes that provide psychiatrists with unprecedented information about the structure and functions of the brain. Computerized tomographic (CT) scanners, the first widely used brain imaging tools, enabled the evaluation of structural brain lesions such as tumors and strokes. Magnetic resonance imaging scans (MRI), introduced later, visualized white and gray matter better than CT scans, making it possible to see smaller brain lesions and white matter abnormalities. In addition to CT and MRI, the evolution of functional imaging has enabled neuroscientists to gain unprecedented insight into the human brain. The most advanced techniques for functional brain imaging are positron emission tomography (PET) and single photon emission computed tomography (SPECT).

The initial observation of structural and functional brain imaging in neuropsychiatric disorders such as Dementia, movement disorders, demyelinating disorders, and epilepsy not only contributed to a better understanding of the physiopathology of neurological and mental diseases but also helped the physicians in complex diagnosis cases. Any changes attributable to brain or spinal cord need imaging of the brain and nerves on a neurological exam. Neurological examination includes mental status, cranial nerves, motor system, motor coordination, sensory system, and reflex components. Examination of the mental state evaluates the state of arousal, attention and motivation, memory, language, visual-spatial function, cognitive set, mood, and emotion. Consultant psychiatrists should consider brain imaging for patients with recent psychosis and acute changes in mental status. Clinical examination is always the priority, and brain imaging is requested based on clinical suspicion of central nervous system (CNS) disorder. Psychiatric research aims to classify patients with mental disorders to facilitate the discovery of neuroanatomical and neurochemical bases of mental illness. Researchers have used functional brain imaging to study groups of patients with mental disorders such as schizophrenia, mood disorders, and anxiety disorders, among other disorders. For example, in schizophrenia, neuropathological volume analyses indicate a decrease in the brain's weight, especially its gray matter. There is a lack of axons and dendrites in the cerebral cortex, and CT and MRI may show compensatory enlargement of the lateral and third ventricles. Especially the temporal lobes of people with schizophrenia seem to have suffered the most significant reduction compared to normal individuals. New studies have shown that the left temporal lobe is affected more than the right temporal lobe.

The frontal lobe may also have abnormalities, but this abnormality is not in the volume of the lobe but in the level of activity observed in functional brain imaging.

Patients with schizophrenia consistently show a decrease in metabolic activity in the frontal lobes, especially while performing tasks requiring the prefrontal cortex activity. Schizophrenic patients are also more likely to exhibit brain ventricle enlargement than non-schizophrenic individuals. Mood and emotional disorders may also be associated with decreased brain volume and metabolic activity in the frontal lobes. Decreasing the activity in the left prefrontal cortex seems to depress the mood, and reducing the activity in the right prefrontal cortex causes the mood to rise. Among anxiety disorders, studies of obsessive-compulsive disorders with conventional CT and MRI methods have shown a lack of specific abnormalities or a reduction in the size of the caudate nucleus.

Functional PET and SPECT studies indicate abnormalities in corticolimbic, basal ganglia, and thalamic nuclei in this disorder. When a patient experiences symptoms of obsessive-compulsive disorder, the prefrontal cortex shows abnormal activity. Relative normalization of glucose metabolism in the caudate nucleus is observed in patients who use drugs such as fluoxetine (Prozac) and clomipramine (Anafranil) or are undergoing behavioral treatments. Functional imaging studies of the brain in patients with attention-deficit/hyperactivity disorder (ADHD) were either regular or showed a reduction in the volume of the right prefrontal cortex and the right globus pallidus.

In addition, in normal conditions, the right caudate nucleus is larger than the left caudate nucleus; in ADHD patients, the size of the caudate nuclei on both sides may be equal. These findings indicate a dysfunction of the prefrontal-striatal pathway for attention control. Early insights into the application of different brain regions were obtained from observations of deficits caused by local injuries, tumors, and strokes. Functional brain imaging has allowed researchers to review and re-evaluate classic teachings on the healthy brain. To date, most research has been in the field of language and vision. Although many unusual features and limitations of PET, SPECT, and Functional magnetic resonance imaging (fMRI) have been studied, none of these methods has a clear superiority over the other. Studies require carefully controlled conditions. However, functional imaging has achieved significant conceptual advances, and today the major limitation of these methods is the creativity of research designs. Studies are designed to understand the functional neuroanatomy of all senses, gross and fine motor skills, language, memory, calculation, learning and thinking disorders, mood, and anxiety. Unconscious feelings that are transmitted by the autonomic nervous system are assigned to different areas of the brain. These analyzes provide a basis for comparison with studies of groups of patients with a particular clinical form. They may lead to better treatments of mental illnesses.

Brain imaging in OCD patients has shown coordination data that suggest dysfunction of neural circuits between the orbitofrontal cortex, caudate nucleus, and thalamus. A variety of functional studies of brain imaging, for example, positron emission tomography (PET), show increased activity (e.g., metabolism and blood flow) in the frontal lobes, basal ganglia (especially the caudate nucleus), and cingulum in patients with OCD. It is said that drug and behavioral treatment will restore these abnormalities. The data obtained from the functional brain imaging studies are consistent with those obtained from the structural brain imaging studies. Both computed tomography and magnetic resonance imaging (MRI) studies have reported a decrease in the size of the caudate nuclei bilaterally in patients with obsessive-compulsive disorder. Both functional and structural brain imaging studies are consistent with the observation that neurological methods on the cingulum are sometimes effective in treating patients with obsessive-compulsive disorder. A MRI study reported increased T1ReLaxation time in the frontal cortex.

This finding is inconsistent with the location of the abnormalities observed in the PET study (Sadock et al ,2007). Brain imaging studies provide evidence, which states that the issue of impaired performance in obsessive-compulsive disorder is probably due to the thalamic circuit of the basal cortical glands of the pre-frontal. Of course, this issue is not only related to a specific part of the brain. Computed tomography and magnetic resonance imaging studies have shown morphological changes in the basal ganglia in individuals with obsessive-compulsive disorder. In addition, positron emission tomography (PET) showed an abnormal metabolic state at a high level of glucose in the caudate nucleus and orbital gyrus of the left of patients with the obsessive-compulsive disorder compared to the control group The relationship between obsessive-compulsive disorder and increased glucose metabolism in the left frontal lobe, right sensorimotor area, both sides of the frontal area, and the anterior cingulate area have also been reported. This consistent cortical hyperactivity in obsessive-compulsive disorder differs from depression and schizophrenia. At the same time, most of the findings are related to the hypofunction of the bilateral cortical part of the frontal part. However, combining behavioral observations with brain imaging may provide a better approach to determining the brain function of patients with OCD and control subjects who have been observed. For example, positron emission mapping has shown that the arousal of symptoms of obsessive-compulsive disorder in these patients is correlated with increased blood flow in the left anterior frontal cortical region and negatively with the activation of the frontal lobe cortical part and shows the changes of two possible side of the effects of obsessive-compulsive disorder symptoms. These techniques have made it possible to detect changes in response to treatment. For example, a study with 18Factors (18F) positron emission tomography (PET) showed that responders to OCD show a significant decrease in the brain glucose metabolism in the right tip of the caudate nucleus compared to pretreatment subjects and also nonresponders and the control group, in which these levels did not change. Similar findings have been reported in other studies. It is interesting to note that the effects of pharmacotherapy or behavioral therapy can be measured with these methods (Montgomery and Zohar, 1999). Evidence from neuroimaging and neurosurgery suggests that OCD correlates with hyperactivity in the frontal-striatal circuits of the brain, which include the orbitofrontal cortex (OFC), anterior cingulate cortex (ACC), caudate nucleus, and thalamus (Baxter et al., 1992; Breiter and Rauch, 1996; Maltby, Tolin, Worhunsky, O'Keefe and Kiehl 2005; Saxena and Rauch, 2000).

Few neuroimaging studies have investigated whether different OCD symptoms are associated with distinct neural activation patterns. Among the healthy control group, viewing images related to washing activated the ventral and dorsal prefrontal regions. This pattern was somewhat different from the activations eliquoted by viewing pictures related to checking and hoarding, each of which was associated with restricted activation of the prefrontal region (Mataix-Cols et al., 2003). A heterogeneous group of OCD patients showed significantly greater activation in the ventromedial prefrontal cortex and right caudate nucleus than healthy controls when they viewed images associated with washing.

This also had different activation patterns when viewing other image categories (Mataix-Cols et al., 2004). However, these studies did not examine the specific relationship between neural activation patterns and contamination symptoms associated with OCD. Rauch et al. (1998) found positive correlations between washout symptom severity and regional cerebral blood flow in the left orbitofrontal cortex (OFC), bilateral anterior cingulate cortex (ACC), and right dorsolateral prefrontal cortex. While viewing pictures related to washing in individuals with OCD, who had contamination symptoms, showed activation in the insula and visual regions (Phillips et al., 2000).

To what extent are the neural findings described above similar to the neural conclusions related to the general emotion of disgust? The studies show a relationship between disgust and basal ganglia activation (Phan, Wager, Taylor and Liberzon, 2002).

Also, the insula has often been mentioned in studies related to disgust, especially the studies in which disgust has been compared to fear, showing a specific relationship between disgust and insula activation (Phillips et al., 1997; Shapira et al., 2003; Sprengelmeyer, Rausch, Eysel and Przuntek, 1998; Wright, He, Shapira, Goodman and Liu, 2004). However, other studies have found that the insula may be active during both fear and disgust (Schafer, Schienle, and Vaitl, 2005; Schienle, Schafer, Stark, Walter, and Vaitl, 2005; Schienle et al., 2002; Stark et al., 2003), some essential studies (for example, Schienle et al., 2002) have reported that the insula is a part of the common affective circuit which is generally activated during the processing of emotions and especially in connection with disgust. Several studies have found a link between amygdala activation and the processing of aversive stimuli, but this link occurs concurrently with insula activation (Schafer et al., 2005; Schienle et al., 2002; Stark et al., 2003).

Phillips et al. (2000) reviewed differences between OCD patients who were primarily washers or checkers and healthy controls viewing images of disgust and washing. In all participants, viewing disgust-related images was associated with activating visual areas and the insula. When viewing pictures of washing, only patients who were primarily washers showed similar activation in visual areas and insula. Shapira et al. (2003) examined the differences between OCD patients who were primarily washers and healthy controls while viewing disgusting and threatening images. Washers (compulsive) showed greater activation in the right insula, parahippocampal region, and inferior frontal regions while viewing disgusting images compared to controls. These groups were not significantly different from each other while watching threatening images. Interestingly, these findings showed the connection between washing symptoms and feelings of disgust (Tolin and Meunier, 2008).

Although there are conflicting reports in this regard, functional neuroimaging studies have mainly focused on showing increased activity of the orbitofrontal cortex and caudate nucleus in OCD (Baxter et al., 1992; Breiter et al., 1996). fMRI and PET studies of OCD patients under symptom arousal during scanning have shown increased regional cerebral blood flow and brain activation in the caudate nucleus and orbitofrontal cortex (Rauch et al., 1994; McGuire et al., 1994; Breiter et al., 1996). Increased activation of the caudate nucleus and anterior orbital frontal cortex is specific to OCD compared to other anxiety states. Interestingly, specific pretreatment functional/metabolic patterns may predict differential response, or lack thereof, into specific therapeutic interventions, for example, SSRIs (serotonin reuptake inhibitors) compared to cognitive behavioral therapy (CBT). Comparable reductions in right caudate nucleus glucose metabolism associated with reductions in OCD symptom severity were investigated before and after ten weeks of treatment with fluoxetine or CBT (Baxter et al., 1992; Schwartz et al., 1996). Before treatment with fluoxetine or CBT, a correlation between the caudate nucleus, orbitofrontal cortex, and thalamus was observed in patients with OCD. However, this correlation was not seen in the control group. After pharmacotherapy or effective CBT, there was no correlation between these areas as in the healthy control group. Patients with OCD who responded to SSRI paroxetine treatment showed a significant decrease in glucose metabolism in the right caudate nucleus and right anterior orbital frontal cortex. Individuals who did not respond to paroxetine treatment did not show a significant decreased glucose metabolism in these areas. Overall, reduced left and right orbitofrontal cortex glucose metabolism of OCD patients before treatment predicted a better response to paroxetine.

Because the clinical phenomenology, classification, and treatment of OCD are well studied, OCD is a particularly suitable case for evaluating appropriate biomarkers (e.g., neuroimaging, genetics). OCD is an excellent example of findings from fundamental neuroscience, neuroimaging, and genetics labs testing advances in treatments, for instance, glutamate-modulating agents. Furthermore, it is a two-way route where findings in the clinic help inform relevant neurobiological studies. There is an exciting future in our efforts to develop new diagnostic and treatment approaches for children's OCD (Rosenberg, Easter, and Michalopoulou 2012).

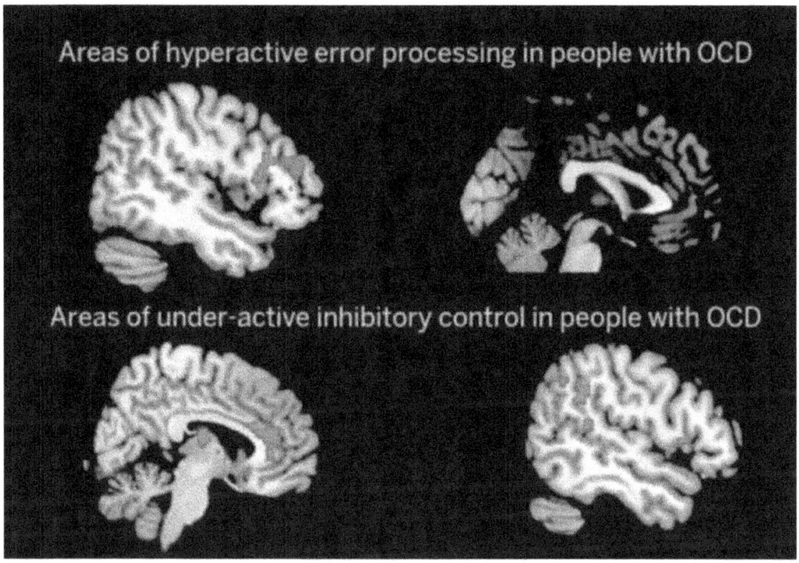

Fig.1. The largest-ever functional imaging study of the brains of people with obsessive-compulsive disorder, and healthy comparison volunteers, shows significant differences in activity in regions involved in error processing and inhibitory control. These images show the regions of the cingulo opercular network where those differences were greatest (Norman, L. J. et al, 2018; Gavin, K. 2018).

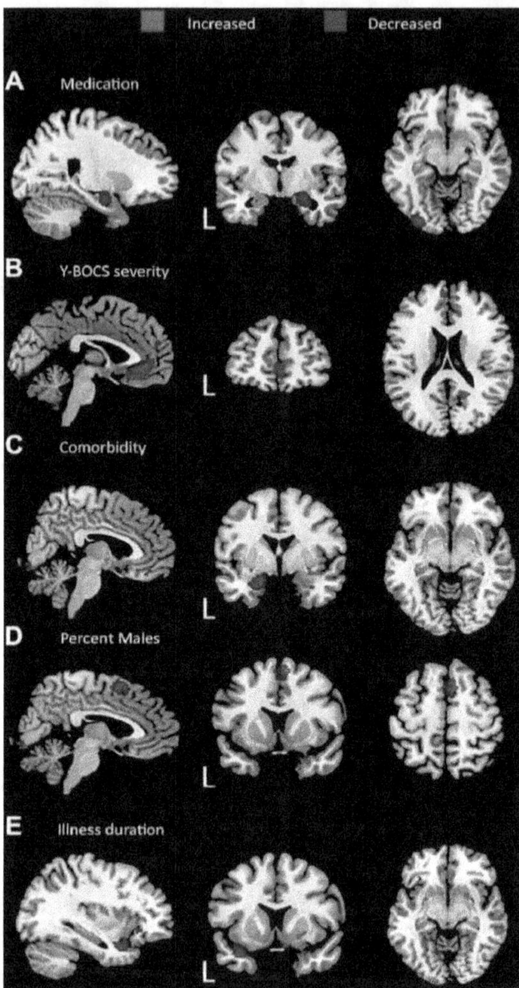

Fig.2. Results of meta-regressions indicating factors that are associated with an increased (red) or decreased (blue) difference between patients with obsessive-compulsive disorder and healthy control subjects.(A) Patient samples with more medicated patients showed less hyperactivation in the right amygdala and left cerebellum. (B) Increased symptom severity correlated with increased patient hyperactivation in the subgenual/rostral anterior cingulate cortex and medial prefrontal cortex. (C) Patient samples with more anxiety and mood disorder comorbidity showed increased activation in the right insula, putamen, and amygdala as well as decreased activation in the left amygdala and right ventromedial prefrontal cortex. (D) Patient samples with more male subjects showed less activation in the presupplementary motor area. (E) Patient samples with longer mean duration of illness showed increased activation in the right putamen and lower activation in the left temporal pole and orbitofrontal cortex. L, left; Y-BOCS, Yale-Brown Obsessive Compulsive Scale.(Thorsen, A. L. et al, 2018).

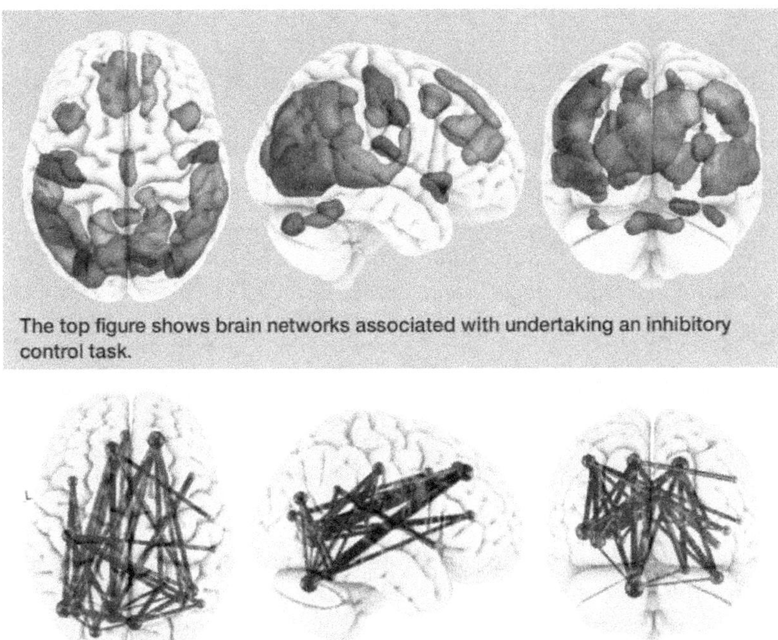

Fig.3. Example of the use of a cognitive task during functional neuroimaging, to explore the neurobiology of OCD.(Hampshire, A. et al, 2020; Grant, J.E. and Chamberlain, S. R. 2020).

8. PHARMACOLOGY OF OCD

More than half of patients with obsessive-compulsive disorder have an acute onset of symptoms. In about 50 to 70 percent of cases, the onset of symptoms occurs after a stressful event, such as pregnancy, sexual issues, or the death of a loved one. Because many patients hide their symptoms, there is often a delay of 5 to 10 years in meeting a psychiatrist. Of course, this delay is decreasing with the increase in individuals' awareness. The process of disorder is usually chronic. In some patients, the symptoms fluctuate; in others, they remain constant. About 20 to 30% of these patients have significant improvement, and 40 to 50% have moderate improvement.

Various reports show that 20 to 40 percent of patients still do not recover or the severity of their symptoms increases daily. Almost one-third of these patients suffer from major depression, and suicide is an essential risk in all these patients. The darker prognosis correlates with the simultaneous presence of major depressive disorder, delusional beliefs, the presence of overvalued ideas (i.e., acceptance of some compulsive and obsessive behavior), the simultaneous presence of a personality disorder (especially schizotypal personality disorder), submission to compulsive behaviors (up to resistance in contrast), childhood-onset, more abnormal obsessive-compulsive behavior and the need for hospitalization. A good prognosis is associated with reasonable occupational and social adjustment, a precipitating event, and the periodic nature of symptoms. Obsessive content has no relation to prognosis.

Due to the growing process indicating that biological factors mainly influence obsessive-compulsive disorder, the classical psychoanalytic theory has lost its importance. In addition, because the symptoms of obsessive-compulsive disorder are resistant to dynamic psychotherapy and psychoanalysis, drug and behavioral treatments have become common. However, psychodynamic factors may have significant advantages in understanding the factors that accelerate the severity of the disorder and the treatment of various types of resistance to treatment, such as non-cooperation in taking medication. Many patients with obsessive-compulsive disorder resist treatment. They may refuse to take medicine and resist doing homework and other activities prescribed by the behavioral therapist. Regardless of their biological origin, obsessive-compulsive symptoms may have an essential psychological meaning that makes the patient hesitate to leave them. Psychodynamic investigation of the patient's resistance to treatment may improve cooperation with treatment. Well-controlled studies have concluded that drug treatment, behavioral therapy, or a combination of the two effectively reduces symptoms in patients with obsessive-compulsive disorder. The treatment decision depends on the physician's judgment and experience and the patient's acceptance of different methods. The effect of pharmacotherapy on obsessive-compulsive disorder has been proven in many clinical trials. The effectiveness of the drug is further confirmed by the fact that studies have shown that the placebo response is about 5%. Medicines, some of which are used to treat depression or other mental disorders, can be prescribed in regular doses. Initial effects usually appear 4 to 6 weeks after starting treatment, although it usually takes 8 to 16 weeks to achieve maximum therapeutic results.

Although treatment with antidepressants is still controversial, in a significant proportion of patients with OCD who respond to antidepressants, the symptoms of the disorder recurrence by discontinuing the treatment, the standard approach is to start treatment with an SSRI (selective serotonin reuptake inhibitor) or clomipramine. If these serotonin-specific drugs are not effective, other treatments are tried. Serotonergic drugs have increased the percentage of patients with obsessive-compulsive disorder likely to respond to treatment to about 50-70%. Each of the SSRIs available in the United States—fluoxetine (Prozac), fluvoxamine (Luvox), paroxetine (Paxil), and sertraline (Zoloft)—is approved for the treatment of OCD by the FDA (World Association of America Food and Drug Administration). Higher doses, such as 80 mg of fluoxetine, are often required for a beneficial effect. Although SSRIs are associated with restlessness, headache, insomnia, nausea and diarrhea, and anxiety, these adverse effects are often temporary and usually less distressing than the side effects of tricyclics, such as clomipramine. The best clinical results are obtained when SSRIs are combined with behavioral therapy.

Among all tricyclic and tetracyclic drugs, clomipramine is more selective for serotonin reuptake versus norepinephrine reuptake, and only SSRIs are superior in this regard. The strength of clomipramine in reabsorbing serotonin is lower than only sertraline and paroxetine. Clomipramine was the first drug accepted by the FDA (World Food and Drug Administration) to treat obsessive-compulsive disorder. To avoid gastrointestinal, intestinal, and orthostatic hypotension adverse effects, the dose of clomipramine should be increased for 2 to 3 weeks. Like other tricyclic drugs, this drug has a significant alleviation and anticholinergic effect, including dry mouth and constipation. Like SSRIs, the best results are obtained from a combination of pharmacotherapy and behavioral therapy. If treatment with clomipramine or an SSRI fails, many therapists augment the first drug with lithium, valproate, or carbamazepine. Other drugs that can be tried in the treatment of obsessive-compulsive disorder are venlafaxine (Effexor) and monoamine oxidase inhibitors (MAOIs), especially phenelzine (Nardil). Other drugs that have been studied in the treatment of resistant patients include buspirone (Buspar), 5-hydroxytryptamine, L-tryptophan, and clonazepam (Klonopin) (Sadock et al ,2007).

In the rest of this chapter, SSRI drugs, tricyclics, and tetracyclics in the treatment of obsessive-compulsive disorder will be discussed.

Selective serotonin reuptake inhibitors

Selective serotonin reuptake inhibitors (SSRIs) are drug choices for treating depression, obsessive-compulsive disorder (OCD), and panic disorder, among many other disorders. Fluoxetine was introduced in 1988 and has been the most commonly prescribed antidepressant worldwide since then. In the following years, sertraline and paroxetine are prescribed almost at a level close to fluoxetine. Fluvoxamine has gained a favorable position, especially for the treatment of OCD. Citalopram has been used in Europe since 1989 and was introduced and approved in the United States in 1998. Escitalopram, an enantiomer of citalopram, is under study in clinical trials. Although depressive disorders were the primary users of these drugs, they are effective in many disorders, including eating disorders, panic disorder, OCD, and borderline personality disorder. These drugs are SSRIs because they share the pharmacodynamic property of explicitly inhibiting serotonin reuptake by presynaptic neurons. They have relatively little effect on the reuptake of norepinephrine and almost no impact on dopamine reuptake.

Clomipramine (Anafranil) is also one of the drugs that act as a serotonin reuptake inhibitor. However, due to the similarity of its chemical structure to antidepressants used to treat depression, it is classified with tricyclic and tetracyclic (antidepressant) drugs. SSRIs do not share molecular characteristics, which is why some individuals may respond to an SSRI and others may not. Fluoxetine, sertraline, paroxetine, and citalopram are used to treat depression. SSRIs are the drug choice for depression in the general population, the elderly, and the physically ill and pregnant women. SSRIs are as effective as other antidepressants for mild to moderate depression. For severe and melancholic depression, several studies have shown that the effect of serotonin-norepinephrine reuptake inhibitors, such as venlafaxine (Effexor), mirtazapine (Remeron), and other tricyclic drugs are often superior to SSRIs. sertraline may be more effective than other SSRIs in treating major melancholic depression. Initiation of treatment with SSRIs is appropriate for all degrees of depression. Direct comparisons of the benefits of different SSRIs have not shown the superiority of one of them over the drugs in their group.

Therefore, an individual may show considerable differences in response to different SSRIs. In conclusion, before changing the drug to a non-SSRI in a person who did not respond to the first SSRI, it is necessary to try another drug from the class of SSRIs. Studies have shown that SSRIs have similar effects but a more favorable adverse effect profile than tricyclic antidepressants. These studies have also consistently demonstrated that patients treated with SSRIs have more significant irritability, sleep disturbance, gastrointestinal symptoms, and possibly sexual side effects than patients treated with tricyclics. Some experts have tried to select a particular SSRI based on its adverse effect profile for specific individuals.

For example, because fluoxetine has the most stimulating and minor alleviation properties, it may be more suitable for lethargic patients. On the contrary, paroxetine has sedative effects. However, these differences usually vary from person to person.

SSRIs significantly reduce the risk of suicide. When these drugs were first introduced, fluoxetine was widely reported to be associated with violent acts, including suicide, but subsequent studies refuted this link. However, few patients experience anxiety and restlessness when taking fluoxetine.

The appearance of these symptoms in a suicidal patient probably makes suicidal thoughts more serious. In addition, suicidal patients may act out suicidal thoughts when they start to come out of depression. Thus, potentially suicidal patients should be carefully monitored during the first few weeks of SSRI therapy. Antidepressants are an essential component of the treatment of suicidal patients. A recent evaluation of the use of drugs to treat individuals with a history of suicide attempts concluded that the majority of them received inadequate doses of antidepressants.

Fluvoxamine, sertraline, paroxetine, and fluoxetine can be prescribed to treat obsessive-compulsive disorder in individuals over 18 years old. Fluvoxamine and sertraline are also approved for treating OCD in children (ages 6-17). About 50% of individuals with OCD show symptoms in childhood and adolescence, and more than half respond positively to medication. The favorable responses may be significant. Long-term data support the model of OCD as a lifespan genetic disorder that is best treated continuously with medicines and cognitive-behavioral therapy from the onset of symptoms in childhood through the end of life. In general, the effective dosages of SSRIs for the treatment of OCD are higher than those required for the treatment of depression, and fluoxetine is effective for OCD at doses of 20, 40, and 60 mg per day. The dose is selected depending on the degree of response.

A 60 mg/day dose is significantly more effective than 20 mg/day. The response to sertraline in OCD is not very dose-dependent, and the drug's effect appears at doses of 50 to 200 mg per day. Paroxetine is effective at doses of 40 and 60 mg/day; 20 mg is no better than a placebo. The response may appear within the first few weeks of treatment, but 15-20% of patients respond after a long treatment. Comorbid depressive symptoms respond significantly more in SSRIs than in clomipramine, nortriptyline, or amitriptyline. Concomitant tics, for example, in tic disorders other than Tourette's, reply to the addition of dopamine receptor antagonists or serotonin dopamine receptor antagonists, such as risperidone.

Conversely, clozapine and buspirone may make tics worse. There appears to be no role in the addition of lithium in treating OCD. The combination of SSRIs and clomipramine is dangerous due to the possibility of cardiotoxicity. SSRIs may effectively treat specific phobias, generalized anxiety disorder, and separation anxiety disorder. The first principle is a comprehensive individual assessment and special attention to the recognition of medically treatable disorders. Cognitive behavioral therapy or other psychotherapies can be added for further improvement.

In 1997, Dexfenfluramine (Redux), a serotonin-releasing agent, was withdrawn from the market due to heart valve defects. This raised concerns about the long-term use of SSRIs. In particular, since both dexfenfluramine and SSRIs somehow increase serotonin activity, could SSRIs also cause valvular heart defects, primary pulmonary hypertension, and serotonergic fiber loss caused by dexfenfluramine? All available evidence suggests that SSRIs do not cause the same adverse effects as dexfenfluramine. Dexfenfluramine causes the release of large amounts of serotonin throughout the body, especially nerve endings, beyond what is needed for standard nerve transmission. High plasma serotonin concentrations are thought to play a role in heart and lung damage.

Conversely, SSRIs prolong the activity of serotonin released into the synaptic cleft during normal neurotransmission. SSRIs do not damage serotonergic fibers and do not increase plasma serotonin concentration. Clinically, SSRIs have been used by a lot of individuals worldwide and have been the subject of much scrutiny. These drugs have not been associated with an increased risk of valvular heart disease or pulmonary hypertension (Sadock et al ,2007).

Tricyclics and Tetracyclics

Tricyclic and tetracyclic antidepressants (commonly abbreviated as TCAs (Tricyclic antidepressants)) are used in treating individuals with a wide range of disorders, including depression, panic disorder, generalized anxiety disorder, post-traumatic stress disorder, obsessive-compulsive disorder, eating disorders, and pain syndromes. With the current availability of selective serotonin reuptake inhibitors (SSRIs), bupropion, nefazodone, venlafaxine, trazodone, and mirtazapine, today TCAs are not widely used to treat the above disorders. Treatment of episodes of major depression and preventive treatment of major depressive disorder are among the primary uses of tricyclic and tetracyclic drugs. These drugs are also effective in treating depression in bipolar I patients.

Melancholic characteristics, previous episodes of major depression, and a family history of depressive disorders increase the probability of treatment response. Treatment of major depressive episodes with psychotic features almost always requires the combined administration of an antipsychotic and an antidepressant. All tricyclics have a tricyclic core in their molecular structure. Imipramine, amitriptyline, clomipramine, trimipramine, and doxepin are tertiary amines because they have two methyl groups on the side nitrogen atom. Desipramine, nortriptyline, and protriptyline are called secondary amines because they have only one methyl group in this site. Tertiary amines are metabolized to their corresponding secondary amines in the body. The classification of tetracyclics is somewhat arbitrary and relies on the total number of rings in their molecular structure. Amoxapine, a dibenzoxazepine derivative of the antipsychotic clozapine and has a cyclic side chain separated from the tricyclic core. Maprotiline is a tetracyclic drug with a side chain similar to desipramine, It's fourth ring actually is a bridge over the central ring of the standard tricyclic core. Mianserin is a tetracyclic drug whose side chain is cyclic to form the tetracyclic.

The obsessive-compulsive disorder appears to respond specifically to clomipramine and SSRIs. None of the tricyclic and tetracyclic drugs seem as effective as clomipramine for this disorder. Multicenter-controlled trials have found clomipramine superior to SSRIs, and another controlled study found paroxetine equivalent to clomipramine in the treatment of the obsessive-compulsive disorder.

Childhood enuresis is often treated with imipramine. Peptic ulcer disease, which has pronounced antihistamine effects, can be treated with doxepin. Other uses of tricyclic and tetracyclic drugs include narcolepsy, nightmare disorder, and post-traumatic stress disorder. These drugs are also used in children with attention-deficit / hyperactivity disorder, somnambulism disorder, separation anxiety disorder, and sleep panic disorder. Clomipramine has been used to treat premature ejaculation, movement disorders, and obsessive behavior in autistic children.

One of the significant adverse effects of tricyclic and tetracyclic antidepressants is the possibility of a manic episode in bipolar I patients and patients with no history of bipolar I disorder. In bipolar I patients, physicians should watch out for the appearance of this complication, primarily if the mania caused by substances has caused difficulties for the patient in the past. In such patients, it is wise to treat with smaller amounts of tricyclic and tetracyclic antidepressants or other drugs such as fluoxetine or bupropion, thus reducing the possibility of manic episodes. Tricyclic and tetracyclic drugs can aggravate psychotic disorders in susceptible patients. Tricyclic and tetracyclic drugs should be avoided during pregnancy. These drugs enter the milk and may cause serious side effects in infants. However, in a series of cases, clomipramine at therapeutic concentrations in lactating women did not produce detectable concentrations in their infants. They should be used with caution in patients with liver and kidney disease. Tricyclic and tetracyclic drugs should not be used during electroconvulsive therapy (ECT), mainly due to serious adverse cardiac effects (Sadock et al, 2007).

Since OCD symptoms increase and decrease, many patients will experience some continuous symptoms that change in severity over time. Some evidence shows that long-term use (pharmacotherapy) may be necessary for some patients who respond to pharmacotherapy. Leonard et al. (1991) conducted a double-blind study of desipramine substitution in patients on long-term clomipramine use. This study showed that 8 out of 9 patients replaced with desipramine had a relapse (to symptoms), while only 2 out of 11 patients who were not replaced had relapses (to symptoms). This finding is confirmed by the study of Pato et al. (1988), in which most adult patients had a recurrence of symptoms after stopping clomipramine.

However, it is recommended to reduce pharmacotherapy to determine its necessity periodically. Usually, for a patient who has shown the symptoms of the disease and has had a positive clinical response, it is not necessary to slowly reduce the use of drugs in the first year.

Patients often do not experience a sudden increase in OCD symptoms; instead, they will have a gradual, harmful relapse (to symptoms) over the next 1 to 3 months. Although many patients respond rapidly to one of the SSRIs, a significant minority do not respond until eight or even 12 weeks of treatment (with therapeutic doses late in treatment).

Therefore, it is important for the physician to patiently determine the therapeutic dose and wait for a response for at least 10 -12 weeks before changing agents or performing enhancement regimens. If there is no clinical response after 12 weeks, another SSRI should be substituted. In a population of children with a tic disorder, adding low-dose haloperidol (1 -3 mg/day) or pimozide (0/5 – 2 mg/day) may be necessary.

In a double-blind placebo-controlled study, McDougle et al. (1994) found that this combination (anti-obesity and a dopamine blocker) was an effective treatment intervention for obsessive-compulsive symptoms and tics, while anti-obesity drugs were not effective alone (Penn and Leonard, 2001).

Table 1. Drug treatment options for the anxiety disorders, OCD and PTSD ; PD: panic disorder; SAD: social anxiety disorder; GAD: generalised anxiety disorder; OCD: obsessive compulsive disorder; PTSD: post-traumatic stress disorder ; SSRI: selective serotonin reuptake inhibitor; SNRI: serotonin and noradrenaline reuptake inhibitor; TCA: tricyclic antidepressant; MAOI: monoamine oxidase inhibitor; NaSSA: noradrenergic and specific serotonergic antidepressant; MASSA: melatonin agonist and specific serotonin antagonist (Outhoff , K. 2016).

Class	Drug	Dose/day	PD	SAD	OCD	GAD	PTSD
SSRI	Paroxetine	20–60 mg	x	x	x	x	x
	Citalopram	20–60 mg	x	x	x		
	Escitalopram	10–20 mg	x	x	x	x	
	Fluoxetine	20–60 mg	x	x	x		x
	Sertraline	25–200 mg	x	x	x	x	x
	Fluvoxamine	50–300 mg	x	x	x		
SNRI	Venlafaxine	75–225 mg	x	x		x	x
	Duloxetine	60–120 mg				x	
TCA	Clomipramine	25–250 mg	x		x		
	Imipramine	25–250 mg	x			x	x
MAOI	Phenelzine	45–90 mg	x	x	x		
MASSA	Agomelatine	25–50 mg				x	
NaSSA	Mirtazapine	30–60 mg			x		x
Benzodiazepine	Alprazolam	1.5–8 mg	x				
	Clonazepam	1–4 mg	x	x			
	Diazepam	5–20 mg	x			x	
	Lorazepam	2–8 mg	x			x	
Anticonvulsant	Pregabalin	150–600 mg				x	
Antipsychotic	Quetiapine	50–300 mg				x	
Azapirone	Buspirone	15–45 mg				x	

REFERENCES

1- Abramowitz JS, Foa EB (1998). Worries and obsessions in individuals with obsessive-compulsive disorder with and without comorbid generalized anxiety disorder. Behav Res Ther 36: 695–700.

2- Abramowitz, J.S. and Foa, E.B. (2000). Does co-morbid major depression influence outcome of exposure and response prevention for OCD? Behaviour Therapy, 31, 795–800.

3- Abudy. Anat , Juven-Wetzler. Alzbeta , Sonnino. Rachel, Zohar. Joseph (2012); Obsessive-Compulsive Disorder, Current Science and Clinical Practice: Chapter 9, Serotonin and beyond: a neurotransmitter perspective of OCD; Wiley-Blackwell, A John Wiley & Sons, Ltd.

4- Ahmari. Susanne E and Rauch. Scott L.; The prefrontal cortex and OCD; Neuropsychopharmacology (2022) 47:211–224.

5- American Academy of Child and Adolescent Psychiatry (AACAP) (2012); Obsessive-Compulsive Disorder in Children and Adolescents; Facts for Families, No. 60.

6- Antony, M. M., Downie, F., & Swinson, R. P. (1998). Diagnostic issues and epidemiology in obsessive compulsive disorder. In R. P. Swinson, M. M. Antony, S. Rachman & M. Richter (Eds.), Obsessive compulsive disorder: Theory, research and treatment (pp. 3-32).New York: Guilford Press.

7- Attiullah N, Eisen JL, Rassmussen SA (2000). Clinical features of obsessive-compulsive disorder. Psych Clin NAm 23: 469–491.

8- Baxter, L. R., Jr., Schwartz, J. M., Bergman, K. S., Szuba, M. P., Guze, B. H., Mazziotta, J. C., Alazraki, A., Selin, C. E., Ferng, H. K., Munford, P., et al. (1992). Caudate glucose metabolic rate changes with both drug and behavior therapy for obsessive-compulsive disorder. Archives of General Psychiatry, 49, 681-689.

9- Breiter HC, Rauch SL, Kwong KK et al. Functional magnetic resonance imaging of symptom provocation in obsessive compulsive disorder. Arch Gen Psychiatry 1996; 53:595–606.

10- Breiter, H. C., & Rauch, S. L. (1996). Functional MRI and the study of OCD: from symptom provocation to cognitive-behavioral probes of cortico-striatal systems and the amygdala. NeuroImage, 4, 127-138.

11- Brosan. Lee, Dickinson. Rebecca, Gunn. Ellie, Hazzard. Laura, Hudda.Sidika , Smith. Kerry (2010); Coping with obsessions and Compulsions; Improving Access to Psychological Therapies (IAPT), Psychological Treatment Service, Cambridge.

12- Bry'nska, A. (1997). Obsessive compulsive disorder in children and adolescents: Literature review. Part 1.Psychiatria Polska, 31(4), 417-428.

13- Coles. Meredith E. , Wirshba. Carle Jordan, Nota. Jacob, Schubert. Jessica, Grunthal Breanna A. ; Obsessive compulsive disorder prevalence increases with latitude ; Journal of Obsessive-Compulsive and Related Disorders 18 (2018) 25–30.

14- Comer, J.S., Kendall, P.C., Franklin, M.E., Hudson, J.L. and Pimentel, S.S. (2004). Obsessing/worrying about the overlap between obsessive–compulsive disorder and generalised anxiety disorder in youth. Clinical Psychology Review, 24, 6, 663–683.

15- Dadfar. Mahbube , Bowlhari. Jafar ,Malakoti. Kazem ,Bayanzadeh. Akbar(2001). Investigating the prevalence of obsessive-compulsive disorder symptoms ; Iranian Journal of Psychiatry and Clinical Psychology (thought and behavior) ,7(1 ,2) 27-33.

16- Davison. Gerald C. , Neale. John M. , Kring. Ann M. (2004). Abnormal Psychology. Wiley; 9th edition.

17- De Alvarenga. Pedro Gomes, Mastrorosa. Rosana Savio, do Rosário. Maria Conceição (2012); Obsessive-Compulsive Disorder in Children and Adolescents; IACAPAP Textbook of Child and Adolescent Mental Health.

18- de Haas R, Nijdam A, Westra TA, Kas MJ, Westenberg HG. Behavioral pattern analysis and dopamine release in quinpirole-induced repetitive behavior in rats. J Psychopharmacol 2011; 25:1712–1719.

19- Diagnostic and statistical manual of mental disorders : DSM-5. - 5th ed., American Psychiatric Association, 2013.

20- do Rosario-Campos MC, Leckman JF, Curi M, et al. A family study of early-onset obsessive compulsive disorder. Am J Med Genet B Neuropsychiatr Genet 2005;136 :92-97.

21- Eapen V, Robertson MM. Tourette Syndrome and Obsessive Compulsive Disorder. In : Encyclopaedia of the Human Brain. San Diego, California, Md: Academic Press 2002: 615-622.

22- Eapen V, Yakely M, Robertson MM. Obsessive Compulsive Disorder and Self injurious Behavior. In: Kurlan R, Marcel Dekker, eds. Handbook of Tourette Syndrome, 2nd ed. NewYork, 2005: 39-88.

23- Eapen. V (2007); Obsessive Compulsive Disorder, Current Understanding and Future Directions: Chapter4, Genetics of OCD: Current Understanding and Future Directions; National Institute of Mental Health and Neuro Sciences, Bangalore, India.

24- Einat H, Szechtman H. Perseveration without hyperlocomotion in a spontaneous alternation task in rats sensitized to the dopamine agonist quinpirole. Physiol Behav 1995;57: 55–59.

25- Eley, T.C., Bolton, D., O'Connor, T.G., Perrin, S., Smith, P. and Plomin, R. (2003). A twin study of anxiety-related behaviours in pre-school children. Journal of Child Psychology and Psychiatry and Allied Disciplines, 44, 7, 945–960.

26- Foa. Edna B. ,Yadin. Elna , Lichner. Tracey K.(2012) ; Exposure and Response (Ritual) Prevention for Obsessive-Compulsive Disorder: Therapist Guide (Treatments That Work) ; Oxford University Press; 2nd edition.

27- Franklin, M. E., & Foa, E. (2002). Cognitive-behavioral treatments for obsessive-compulsive disorder. In P. E. Nathan & J. M. Gorman (Eds.), A guide to treatments that work (pp. 367–386). Oxford: Oxford University Press.

28- Gavin. Kara; Stuck in a loop of wrongness: Brain study shows roots of OCD ; Michigan Medicine - University of Michigan , Biological Psychiatry , 2018.

29- Geller, D. A., Biederman, J., Jones, J., Shapiro, S.,Schwartz, S., & Park, K. S. (1998). Obsessive compulsive disorder in children and adolescents: A review. Harward Review of Psychiatry, 5(5), 260-273.

30- Geller, D.A., Biederman, J., Jones, J., Shapiro, S., Schwartz, S. and Park, K.S. (1998). Obsessive-compulsive disorder in children and adolescents: a review. Harvard Review of Psychiatry, 5, 5, 260–273.

31- Gournay, K. (2006). Assessment and management of obsessive compulsive disorder. Nursing Standard, 20(33),59-65.

32- Graat , I. , Figee, M., & Denys, D. (2017). Neurotransmitter Dysregulation in OCD. Obsessive-Compulsive Disorder: Phenomenology, Pathophysiology, and Treatment. 25, 271-274. United States: Oxford University Press. Christopher Pittenger.

33- Grados. Marco, Prazak. Michael, Saif. Aneeqa & Halls. Andrew ; A review of animal models of obsessive compulsive disorder: a focus on developmental, immune, endocrine and behavioral models; Expert Opin. Drug Discov. (2016) 11(1):27-43.

34- Grant, JD. Jon E. and Chamberlain. Samuel R.; Exploring the Neurobiology of OCD , PsychiatricTimes, www.psychiatrictimes.com , 2020.

35- Hampshire A , Zadel A , Sandrone S, et al. Inhibitionrelated cortical hypoconnectivity as a candidate vulnerability marker for obsessive-compulsive disorder; Biol Psychiatry, 2020, 5(2):222-230.

36- Hanna, G.L., Piacentini, J., Cantwell, D.P., Fischer, D.J., Himle, J.A. and Van Etten, M. (2002). Obsessive-compulsive disorder with and without tics in a clinical sample of children and adolescents. Depression and Anxiety, 16, 2, 59–63.

37- Hasler G, LaSalle-Ricci VH, Ronquillo JG, et al. (2005). Obsessive-compulsive disorder symptom dimensions show specific relationships to psychiatric comorbidity. Psychiatry Res 135 ,121–132.

38- Herbenson. Kristi(2009); Obsessive-Compulsive Disorder: An Overview for School Personnel; A Research Paper Submitted in Partial Fulfillment of the Requirements for the Master of Science Degree in School Counseling , The Graduate School University of Wisconsin-Stout.

39- Heyman, I., Fombonne, E., Simmons, H., Ford, T., Meltzer, H. and Goodman, R. (2001). Prevalence of obsessive-compulsive disorder in the British nationwide survey of child mental health. *British Journal of Psychiatry, 179*, 324–329.

40- Hilgard. Ernest, Atkinson. Richard C., Atkinson. Rita L.(2014) ; Atkinson & Hilgard's Introduction to Psychology ; Wadsworth Pub Co , 16th edition.

41- Hollander E, Greenwald S, Neville D et al. Uncomplicated and comorbid obsessive–compulsive disorder in an epidemiological sample. Depress Anxiety, 1996;7, 4: 111–19.

42- Hudak. Robert (2011); Clinical Obsessive-Compulsive Disorders in Adults and Children: Chapter1, Introduction to obsessive-compulsive disorder; Cambridge university press.

43- Kamath P, Janardhan Reddy YC, Kandavel T (2007). Suicidal behavior in obsessive-compulsive disorder. J Clin Psychiatry 68: 1741–1750.

44- Karpinski. Marta, Mattina. Gabriella Francesca , Steiner. Meir; Effect of Gonadal Hormones on Neurotransmitters Implicated in the Pathophysiology of Obsessive-Compulsive Disorder: A Critical Review ; Neuroendocrinology, 2017,105:1–16.

45- Kaye WH, Bulik CM, Thornton L, Barbarich N, Masters K (2004). Comorbidity of anxiety disorders with anorexia and bulimia nervosa. Am J Psychiatry 161: 2215–2221.

46- Keeley, M. L., Storch, E. A., Merlo, L. J., & Geffken, G. R. (2008). Clinical predictors of response to cognitive-behavioral therapy for obsessive–compulsive disorder. Clinical Psychology Review, 28, 118–130.

47- Krochmalik. Annette, Menzies. Ross G (2003); Obsessive-Compulsive Disorder. Theory, Research and Treatment: Chapter1, the Classification and Diagnosis of Obsessive-Compulsive Disorder; John Wiley & Sons Ltd, England.

48- Lensi, P., Cassano, G.B., Correddu, G., Ravagli, S., Kunovac, J.L. and Akiskal, H.S. (1996). Obsessive-compulsive disorder: familial-developmental history,symptomatology, co-morbidity and course with special reference to gender-related differences. *British Journal of Psychiatry, 169*, 101–107.

49- Lipsitz JD, Mannuzza S, Chapman TF, et al. A direct interview family study of obsessive compulsive disorder. II. Contribution of proband informant information. Psychol Med.2005; 35:1623-1631.

50- Maltby, N., Tolin, D. E, Worhunsky, E, O'Keefe, T. M., & Kiehl, K. A. (2005). Dysfunctional action monitoring hyperactivates frontal-striatal circuits in obsessive-compulsive disorder: an event-related fMRI study. NeuroImage, 24, 495-503.

51- March, J.S., Foa., E., Gammon, P., Chrisman, A., Curry, J., Fitzgerald, D., et al. (2004). Cognitive-behaviour therapy, sertraline and their combination for children and adolescents with obsessive-compulsive disorder. The Pediatric OCD treatment study (POTS) randomised controlled trial. Journal of the American Medical Association, 292, 1969–1976.

52- Mataix-Cols, D., Cullen, S., Lange, K., Zelaya, F., Andrew, C., Amaro, E., Brammer, M. J., Williams,S. C., Speckens, A., & Phillips, M. L. (2003). Neural correlates of anxiety associated with obsessive compulsive symptom dimensions in normal volunteers. Biological Psychiatry, 53, 482-493.

53- Mataix-Cols, D., Wooderson, S., Lawrence, N., Brammer, M. J., Speckens, A., & Phillips, M. L. (2004). Distinct neural correlates of washing, checking, and hoarding symptom dimensions in obsessive-compulsive disorder. Archives of General Psychiatry, 61,564-576.

54- McGrath MJ, Campbell KM, Parks CR, Burton FH. Glutamatergic drugs exacerbate symptomatic behavior in a transgenic model of comorbid

Tourette's syndrome and obsessive -compulsive disorder. Brain Res 2000; 877:23–30.

55- McGuire PK, Bench CJ, Frith CD et al. Functional anatomy of obsessive-compulsive phenomena. Br J Psychiatry 1994; 164:459–468.

56- Milani Far. Behrouz (2019); Psychology of exceptional children and adolescents; Tehran: Qoms.

57- Mohammadi , M. R., Davidian, H., Noorbala, A. A. , et al (2005). An epidemiological survey of psychiatric disorders in Iran; Clin Pract Epidemiol Ment Health , 1: 16.

58- Montgomery. Stuart , Zohar. Joseph ;Obsessive compulsive disorder ;London: M. Dunitz , 1999.

59- Murphy. Dennis L., Timpano. Kiara R., Wheaton. Michael G., Greenberg Benjamin D., Miguel. Euripedes C.; Obsessive-compulsive disorder and its related disorders: a reappraisal of obsessive-compulsive spectrum concepts; Dialogues in Clinical Neuroscience - Vol 12. No. 2. 2010.

60- Norman. Luke J., et al ; Frontostriatal Dysfunction During Decision Making in Attention-Deficit/Hyperactivity Disorder and Obsessive-Compulsive Disorder; Biological Psychiatry: Cognitive Neuroscience and Neuroimaging , 2018.

61- O'Kearney, R.T., Anstey, K.J. and von Sanden, C. (2006). Behavioural and cognitive behavioural therapy for obsessive compulsive disorder in children and adolescents. Cochrane Database of Systematic Reviews, 4, art. no.: CD004856. DOI: 10.1002/14651858. CD004856.pub2.

62- Outhoff K.; An update on the pharmacological treatment of anxiety and related disorders ; South African Family Practice , 2016, 58(5):50-56.

63- Pauls, D.L., Alsobrook, J.P., Goodman, W., Rasmussen, S. and Leckman, J.F. (1995). A family study of obsessive-compulsive disorder. *American Journal of Psychiatry*, *152*, 76–84.

64- Pauls, D.L., Alsobrook, J.P., Goodman, W., Rasmussen, S. and Leckman, J.F. (1995). A family study of obsessive-compulsive disorder. American Journal of Psychiatry, 152, 76–84.

65- Pauls. David L., Abramovitch. Amitai , Rauch. Scott L. and Geller. Daniel A ; Obsessive–compulsive disorder: an integrative genetic and neurobiological perspective; Article in Nature Reviews Neuroscience ; 2014.

66- Penn. Joseph V, Leonard. Henrietta L (2001); Current Treatments of Obsessive-Compulsive Disorder: Chapter8, Diagnosis and Treatment in

Children and Adolescents; American Psychiatric Publishing, Inc. Washington, DC, London, England.

67- Phan, K. L., Wager, T., Taylor, S. E, & Liberzon, I. (2002). Functional neuroanatomy of emotion: a meta-analysis of emotion activation studies in PET and fMRI. NeuroImage ,16, 331-348.

68- Phillips, M. L., Marks, I. M., Senior, C., Lythgoe, D., O'Dwyer, A. M., Meehan, O., Williams, S. C., Brammer, M. J., Bullmore, E. T., & McGuire, E K. (2000). A differential neural response in obsessive-compulsive disorder patients with washing compared with checking symptoms to disgust. Psychological Medicine, 30, 1037-1050.

69- Phillips, M. L., Young, A. W., Senior, C., Brammer, M., Andrew, C., Calder, A. J., Bullmore, E. T., Perrett, D. I., Rowland, D., Williams, S. C., Gray, J. A., & David, A. S. (1997). A specific neural substrate for perceiving facial expressions of disgust. Nature, 389, 495-498.

70- Pigott TA(1998) Obsessive-compulsive disorder: symptom overview and epidemiology.B Menninger Clin 62:A4–A32.

71- Rachman , S. (1997). A cognitive theory of obsessions. Behaviour Research and Therapy, 35, 793– 802.

72- Rasmussen, S.A. and Eisen, J.L. (1992). The epidemiology and clinical features of obsessive-compulsive disorder. *Psychiatric Clinics of North America*, *15*, 743–758.

73- Rauch SL, Jenike MA, Alpert NM et al. Regional cerebral blood flow measured during symptom provocation in obsessive-compulsive disorder using oxygen 15- labeled carbon dioxide and positron emission tomography. Arch Gen Psychiatry 1994; 51:62–70.

74- Reis. Noah A.; Intracellular Signaling and Neurotransmission Abnormalities Implicated in Obsessive-Compulsive Disorder: A Review; University of California, Santa Barbara , PSY 115, 2020.

75- Roberts Stoler. Diane; Neuromodulators and Neurotransmitters; © 2021 DR. DIANE® ROBERTS STOLER, ED.D.

76- Rosenberg. David R, Easter. Phillip C, Michalopoulou. Georgia (2012); Obsessive-Compulsive Disorder, Current Science and Clinical Practice: Chapter 10, Brain Imaging; Wiley-Blackwell, A John Wiley & Sons, Ltd.

77- Rothstein JD, Martin LJ, Kuncl RW. Decreased glutamate transport by the brain and spinal cord in amyotrophic lateral sclerosis. N Engl J Med 1992;326: 1464–1468.

78- Sadock. Benjamin J. , Kaplan. Harold I., Sadock. Virginia A. (2007) ; Kaplan & Sadock's Synopsis of Psychiatry: Behavioral Sciences/clinical Psychiatry ; Lippincott Williams & Wilkins , 9th edition.

79- Salehi. Mansour, Salari Far. Mohammad Hossein, Hadian. Mina (2004); Evaluaion of the frequency pattern of obsessive-compulsive disorder symptoms; News of cognitive sciences; 6(1, 2) 87-94.

80- Salkovskis , P. M. (1999). Understanding and treating obsessive-compulsive disorder. Behaviour Research and Therapy, 37, 29–52.

81- Salkovskis, P. M. (1998). Psychological approaches to the understanding of obsessional problems. In R. P. Swinson, M. M. Anthony, S. Rachman, & M. A. Richter (Eds.), Obsessive compulsive disorder: Theory, research and treatment (pp. 33–50). New York: Guilford Press.

82- Salkovskis, P.M. (1996). Understanding of obsessive-compulsive disorder is not improved by redefining it as something else: Reply to Pigott et al. and to Enright. In R.M. Rapee (ed.) Current controversies in the anxiety disorders (pp. 191–200). New York: Guilford Press.

83- Saraiva. Leonardo Cardoso, Cappi. Carolina, Simpson. Helen Blair, et al ; Cutting-edge genetics in obsessive-compulsive disorder ; Faculty Reviews, 2020, 9:(30).

84- Saxena, S., & Rauch, S. L. (2000). Functional neuroimaging and the neuroanatomy of obsessive compulsive disorder. Psychiatric Clinics of North America, 23, 563-586.

85- Schafer, A., Schienle , A., & Vaitl, D. (2005). Stimulus type and design influence hemodynamic responses towards visual disgust and fear elicitors. International Journal of Psychophysiology, 57, 53-59.

86- Schaller JL, Behar D, Chamberlain T. When fluvoxamine treats only depression and clomipramine treats only obsessive–compulsive disorder combine them? J Neuropsych Clin Neurosci , 1998; 10: 111–13.

87- Schatzberg AF, Samson JA, Rothschild AJ et al. McLean Hospital Depression Research Facility: early-onset phobic disorders and adult onset major depression. Br J Psychiatry , 1998; 173(suppl 34): 29–34.

88- Schienle, A., Schafer, A., Stark, R., Walter, B., & Vaitl, D. (2005). Neural responses of OCD patients towards disorder-relevant, generally disgust-inducing and fear-inducing pictures. International Journal of Psychophysiology, 57, 69-77.

89- Schienle, A., Stark, R., Walter, B., Blecker, C., Ott, U., Kirsch, E, Sammer, G., & Vaitl, D. (2002). The insula is not specifically involved in disgust processing: an fMRI study. Neuroreport, 13, 2023-2026.

90- Schwartz JM, Stoessel PW, Baxter LR et al. Systematic changes in cerebral glucose metabolic rate after successful behavior modification treatment of obsessive compulsive disorder. Arch Gen Psychiatry 1996;53:109–113.

91- Shafran. Roz (2005); Concepts and Controversies in Obsessive-Compulsive Disorder: Chapter13, Cognitive-Behavioral Models of OCD; Springer Science+ Business Media, Inc.

92- Shams. Gitti, Karam Qadiri. Narges, Ismaili Turkanpuri.Yaqoub, et al (2007); Prevalence of obsessive-compulsive symptoms in teenagers and its comorbidity with other psychiatric symptoms; New Cognitive Sciences, 9(4) , 50-59.

93- Shapira, N. A., Liu, Y., He, A. G., Bradley, M. M., Lessig, M. C., James, G. A., Stein, D. J., Lang, P. J., & Goodman, W. K. (2003). Brain activation by disgust-inducing pictures in obsessive-compulsive disorder. Biological Psychiatry, 54, 751-756.

94- Sharma. Eesha , Sharma. Lavanya P., Balachander. Srinivas ,et al; Comorbidities in Obsessive-Compulsive Disorder Across the Lifespan: A Systematic Review and Meta-Analysis; Frontiers in Psychiatry; 2021.

95- Shear, K.A., Jin, R., Ruscio, A.M., Walters, E.E. and Kessler, R.C. (2006). Prevalence and correlates of estimated DSM-IV child and adult separation anxiety disorder in the national co-morbidity survey replication. American Journal of Psychiatry, 163, 1074–1083.

96- Solmi. Marco, Radua. Joaquim , Olivola. Miriam , et al. Age at onset of mental disorders worldwide: large-scale meta analysis of 192 epidemiological studies; Molecular Psychiatry (2022) 27:281–295.

97- Sprengelmeyer, R., Rausch, M., Eysel, U. T., & Przuntek, H. (1998). Neural structures associated with recognition of facial expressions of basic emotions. Proceedings: Biological Sciences, 265, 1927-1931.

98- Stanley, M. A., & Turner, S. M. (1995). Current status of pharmacological and behavioral treatment of obsessive-compulsive disorder. Behavior Therapy, 26, 163–186.

99- Stark, R., Schienle, A., Walter, B., Kirsch, P., Sammer, G., Ott, U., Blecker, C., & Vaitl, D. (2003). Hemodynamic responses to fear and disgust-inducing pictures: an fMRI study. International Journal of Psychophysiology, 50, 225-234.

100- Stein. Dan J, Hollander. Eric (2003); Anxiety Disorders Comorbid with Depression; Taylor & Francis e-Library.

101- Stein. Dan J., Costa. Daniel L.C., Lochner. Christine, Miguel. Euripedes C. , Reddy. Y. C. Janardhan , Shavitt. Roseli G., van den Heuvel. Odile A.,

Simpson. H. Blair; Obsessive–compulsive disorder; Nat Rev Dis Primers. , 5(1): 52; 2020.

102- Strom. Nora I., Soda. Takahiro, Mathews.Carol A. and Davis. Lea K. ; A dimensional perspective on the genetics of obsessive compulsive disorder ;Translational Psychiatry (2021) 11:401.

103- Sullivan RM, Talangbayan H, Einat H, Szechtman H. Effects of quinpirole on central dopamine systems in sensitized and non-sensitized rats. Neuroscience 1998; 83:781–789.

104- Szechtman H, Eckert MJ, Tse WS et al. Compulsive checking behavior of quinpirole sensitized rats as an animal model of Obsessive-Compulsive Disorder (OCD): form and control. BMC Neurosci 2001;2:4.

105- Thomsen, P.H. (1999). From thoughts to obsessions: obsessive compulsive disorders in children and adolescents, D. Christophersen, trans. London: Jessica Kingsley Publishers.

106- Thorsen. Anders Lillevik , et al ; Emotional Processing in Obsessive-Compulsive Disorder: A Systematic Review and Meta-analysis of 25 Functional Neuroimaging Studies ; Biological Psychiatry: Cognitive Neuroscience and Neuroimaging , 2018.

107- Tolin. David F, Meunier. Suzanne A (2008); Subtypes of Obsessive-Compulsive Disorder: Chapter1, Contamination and Decontamination; Elsevier Ltd.

108- Torres AR, Ramos-Cerqueira AT, Torresan RC, et al. (2007). Prevalence and associated factors for suicidal ideation and behaviors in obsessive-compulsive disorder. CNS Spectr 12: 711–718.

109- Torres, A.R., Prince, M.J., Bebbington, P.E., Bhugra, D.K., Brugha, T.S., Farrell, M., *et al.* (2007). Treatment seeking by individuals with obsessive-compulsive disorder from the British Psychiatric Morbidity Survey of 2000. *Psychiatric Services, 58*, 977–982.

110- Tükel R, Polat A, Ozdemir O, Aksut D, Turksoy N (2002). Comorbid conditions in obsessive-compulsive disorder. Compr Psychiatry 43: 204–209.

111- Weissman MM, Bland RC, Canino GJ & Greenwald S (1994) the cross national epidemiology of obsessive compulsive disorder: the Cross National Collaborative Group. J Clin Psychiat 55(suppl 3):5–10.

112- Williams. Tim I. & Shafran. Roz; Obsessive–compulsive disorder in young people; BJPsych Advances (2015), vol. 21, 196–205.

113- Williams. Tim, Waite. Polly (2009); Obsessive Compulsive Disorder, Cognitive Behaviour Therapy with Children and Young People: Chapter1,

Introduction to obsessive compulsive disorder; Routledge, Taylor & Francis Group, London and New York.

114- Wright, P., He, G., Shapira, N. A., Goodman, W. K., & Liu, Y. (2004). Disgust and the insula: fMRI responses to pictures of mutilation and contamination. Neuroreport, 15, 2347-2351.

115- Zepf, B. (2004). Management strategies for obsessive-compulsive disorder. American Family Physician, 70(7), 1379-1380.

116- Zitterl W, Demal U, Aigner M et al. Naturalistic course of obsessive compulsive disorder and comorbid depression: Longitudinal results of a prospective follow-up study of 74 actively treated patients. Psychopathology , 2000; 33: 75–80.

117- Zohar, A.H. (1999). The epidemiology of obsessive-compulsive disorder in children and adolescents. Child and Adolescent Psychiatric Clinics of North America, 8, 445–460.